WORLD
HISTORY

WORLD HISTORY

MARTIN BALLARD

GEDDES&
GROSSET

First published 1992
© 1992 Geddes & Grosset Ltd,
New Lanark, Scotland.

Cover design by Cameron Graphics Ltd,
Glasgow, Scotland.

ISBN 1 85534 094 1

Printed and bound in Great Britain.

Contents

1. Early Civilizations of Asia.

Before History.

Origins. Scientists estimate that the earth was formed some 4600 million years ago. Fossils of the simplest animals and plants have been found in rocks dating from 1000 million years later. The early development of life within those ancient seas was inconceivably slow. The first land plants and animals evolved in the Silurian age, over 400 million years ago. The great dinosaurs ruled the earth for the 160 million years of the Mesozoic Era, which ended some 65 million years BC. The extinction of these giants provided the opportunity for the family of mammals to begin their colonization of the planet.

Some two million years ago several groups of primates, living around the forest edge in Africa, began to show characteristics which might be called 'human'. These creatures began to plan their hunting expeditions and their use of weapons. Other animals use tools – no other animals make tools for something they plan to do tomorrow!

Still, the development of man into the species *homo*

sapiens remained immensely slow. Some evolutionary pathways proved to be dead ends. But the spread of the family of man was relentless. For hundreds of thousands of years, small bands of these evolving people moved into new environments, hunting and gathering their food as they went. The animal, man, proved remarkably adaptable, surviving the cold of the ice ages and the heat of the tropics.

The First Agricultural Revolution. The last ice age rolled back some 12,000 years ago, leaving the world with much the same climate that it has retained until today. Comparatively shortly afterwards some people began to introduce major changes into the timeless pattern of life.

Wild wheat and barley live naturally in the area between eastern Turkey and the Caspian Sea. At some time people -probably the women – learnt that it was possible to plant the seeds and so reduce the work of gathering. Soon these new farmers began to select which seeds produced the best crop, and so improved the quality of the crops.

The introduction of cereal farming had radical effects on human life. Tribal groups lost their mobility as they had to settle in one place to tend the crops. When, in time, one group began to produce a surplus, it had to defend its goods against attack. Settlements then needed to be fortified and a military class grew up within the community. Once a community was producing a surplus of food, some people could undertake specialised roles within the community.

The domestication of animals was, no doubt, a long process. There was no sharp dividing line between the time when the people followed herds of wild animals as hunters, and the time when they drove the animals as herders. During the same years after the last ice age, people of southern Asia and Europe domesticated sheep, cattle and pigs. In the millennia that followed, tribesmen from the mountains of northern Iran and the steppes of Central Asia tamed the horse and camel.

Scholars differ about the pattern of development of settled agriculture. The traditional view was that all innovation happened in the Fertile Crescent of the Middle East, and skills spread outward, like ripples on a pond. Others hold that settled agriculture was discovered in many different places as conditions favoured it. Certainly the new methods appeared across Europe, as well as in India and Africa in the millennia which followed. Developments in the Far East and the Americas, at least, were independent of those in the Fertile Crescent. Millet and rice were cultivated in China and South East Asia from about 6000 BC. Here chicken, water buffalo and, again, pigs were domesticated. Change came later in the Americas, where maize, the potato and other important crops were added to the world's store.

The Growth of Cities.

As the agricultural age continued, so people began to gather into yet larger communities. The earliest discovered is Jericho, which grew up before 8000 BC. Two thousand years later, Catal Hüyük, in Anatolia, covered 32 acres. These cities provided protection and allowed for greater specialization of role for the inhabitants.

New skills were, indeed, needed. Copper was smelted in Anatolia in about 7000 BC, introducing the age of metals. The earliest known pottery and evidence of the first woollen textiles have both been found in Catal Hüyük.

City life also provided a centre for religious worship. A temple lay at the heart of the community, and religion and government were always closely allied to each other. The change in lifestyle brought with it a change in religious practice. Cave paintings, such as those of southern France give a glimpse of the cults of the hunter gatherers, which focused on animals and sacred places. These have much in common with the practices of people, like some North American Indians, who lived similar lives within historical times.

Settled agriculture brought with it a new emphasis on birth and fertility, symbolised by the mother goddess figures found from widely dispersed areas of this early civilized world.

Sumerian Civilization.

Irrigation. As would be expected, the earliest developments in city life happened in regions which had adequate natural rainfall. Some time after 5000 BC, however, groups from the north began to settle in the dry land of Mesopotamia. Here they drained the marshes and used the water from the twin rivers Tigris and Euphrates to irrigate the fertile land.

The Rise of the Sumerian Cities. It appears as though two of the most vital inventions in the history of man – the wheel and the plough – were made in Mesopotamia in around 3500 BC. These enabled farmers to cultivate the irrigated land in a more concentrated manner, so increasing the surplus production, leading to a spectacular flourishing of cities.

The most famous city, Ur of the Chaldes, was only one; also prominent were Eridu, Uruk, Bad-tibira, Nippur and Kish. Each city had its own special deity, and it served as the centre for a surrounding region of villages and farm land.

The Invention of Writing. In about 3100 BC the people of these Sumerian cities learnt how to represent their spoken language by the use of writing. The earliest characters were pictographic, and remain largely undeciphered. The Sumerians later developed the more flexible cuneiform script. The invention of writing marks the beginning of history, but the earliest documents were unremarkable. Written on the tablets of clay are lists showing the ownership of jars of oil and bundles of reeds. They do show, however, that some of the inhabitants were gathering serious wealth, which could be measured in hundreds and thousands of units.

Life in Sumeria. The cities were walled, but it appears that, in the early centuries, this was not a world of warring cities. Disputes were controlled by the exchange of embassies and by dynastic marriages, rather than by conflict. The laws which governed behaviour were not particularly strict.

The area was short of both wood and stone, and the Sumerian people depended heavily on clay for building and many other functions. The skills of the artisans became ever more refined. Gold, silver, bronze and polished stones were made into fine objects for the decoration of people, homes and temples. Weavers, leather workers and potters followed their specialised crafts. The scribes of later centuries wrote down a fine oral tradition of myths, epics and hymns. The world in The world in which small family groups of hunters lived in co-operation had now been left far behind. Everyday life was controlled by a highly developed bureaucracy, which – for good or ill – was to become a hall-mark of civilization. Kings were now divine beings, who were buried, not only with treasure, but also with their whole retinue to see them into the next life.

Egypt.

In about 3200 BC King Menes united the whole of the land of the lower Nile. The deserts which stretched on both sides of the river largely protected the Egyptians against the invasions which plagued Mesopotamia. Egyptian rulers had to face the armies of Assyria and 'The People of the Sea' from the Mediterranean, but the remarkable endurance of Egyptian civilization owes much to its isolation. Despite this, the Egyptians owed much to the Sumerians. In particular, they borrowed the early Sumerian system of writing, and adapted this into their own pictorial script. *Hieroglyphics* means 'the writing of the priests' and the art remained a closely guarded secret within the priestly caste.

For more than 2000 years dynasties followed one another; the country experienced bad times as well as good, but a continuity was maintained, unparalleled in the history of the world. Even when the land later fell under foreign rulers, Egyptian culture retained its remarkable integrity.

The Nile Waters. Egypt depended on the Nile. This was a kindlier river than the Tigris and Euphrates because each year it flooded the land on either side, providing natural irrigation for the fertile soil. The whole of Egyptian life was attuned to the rise and fall of the great river. The ruler – or pharaoh, as he would later be called – was the owner of the land and the giver of its life, and the ceremonials of kingship centred on the fertility of the land. The Book of Exodus describes how the rulers of Egypt were able to organize the storage of surpluses from good years to guard against crop failures in bad years.

The Calendar. The Egyptians studied the movements of the sun and stars, and they were the first to work out the year, consisting of 364¼ days. For the Egyptian farmer, this year was divided into three parts, each of four months – one of flooding, one of planting and one of harvesting.

The Capital Cities. Menes set up his capital in Memphis. Later pharaohs moved it to Thebes, but neither were true cities, like those of Sumeria. Their role was more as a centre of religion than a focus for daily life.

The wide deserts provided more protection from enemies than any city walls. Because of this physical isolation, Egyptian life could remain focused on the villages, rather than on larger centres of population.

Monuments and Art. The massive monuments of ancient Egypt remain objects of wonder. Imhotep, builder of the Step Pyramid at Saqqara, has left his name as the first architect known to history. Many thousands were marshalled to build these tombs for the rulers, working without winches, pulleys, blocks or tackles.

A modern visitor will look with awe at the pyramids and other great stone monuments, but it is the more modest paintings which give insight into the daily lives of the people. They show scenes of busy rural life, where peasants gather crops and hunt wild fowl by the Nile. They are happily free from the scenes of carnage and inhumanity, which is all too common in much of the art of the period. It was a world in which women had a high status and beauty was admired.

No doubt the peasants had to work hard to keep not only themselves but the whole apparatus of royal and priestly rule, but the river was kind and the land was fertile, and there was usually enough for all.

Migration and Trade.

Semites and Indo Europeans. The Semites were herders of sheep who originated in the Arabian peninsula. They were a warrior people, reared in the stern disciplines of life at the desert edge. The most powerful group in those early years them were a people called the Amorites. They founded cities to the north of Sumeria – Babylon, Nineveh and Damascus. The Indo-Europeans were mainly cattle herders, who made their way into Mesopotamia from the north. Their gods emerge in the Pantheon of Greece and in the Vedic deities of India.

The Indo-Europeans had learned how to tame horses from their Asian neighbours. Most importantly, they brought iron. Iron weapons and chariots gave them a technological advantage over the earlier inhabitants of Mesopotamia. Control of iron therefore became an es-

sential precondition of political power. The slow spread
of iron technology had other important effects. An iron
plough could break in land which had hitherto been too
hard for agriculture. This created a rise in production, and
hence an increase in population.

The Growth of Trade. Newcomers from both north
and south were drawn into Mesopotamia by the rich life
style of the cities. But it happened that the area had no
significant iron deposits, and was generally poor in other
metals. This urgent need for raw materials was to be the
driving force for the development of trade in the ancient
world.

Money. It is remarkable how much trade was carried
on before the development of currency as a method of
exchange. Merchants from the civilized Fertile Crescent
were able to take a range of manufactured goods to
exchange for metals and other raw materials. Goods
were also moved around the world as tribute, taxes and
offerings to temples. The first coins date from about 700
BC , but their use spread slowly. Egypt, for instance, did
not introduce a currency until about 400 BC.

Land Transport. The wheel was of no value in a
world without roads. Columns of pack animals began to
spread out from the Near East into the highlands of Iran
and, through the Balkans, into metal rich Europe, opening up trade routes which would be trampled for many
centuries.

Sea Transport. Improvements in the design of ships followed. Oars and sails were developed and rigging improved; decks were made watertight. The Red Sea and Persian Gulf became navigable all the year round, and the Mediterranean at least in summer. The growth in sea transport would ultimately change the centre of gravity of early civilizations away from the inland rivers towards the coastal regions. Ideas and empires could now spread along sea as well as land routes.

Against this background, the empires of the ancient Near East rose and fell.

Babylon, Assyria and the Hittites.

Babylon. In 1792 BC a ruler called Hammurabi came to power in the Semite city of Babylon. He can be looked upon as the first great emperor in the history of the world. Hammurabi's armies carried Babylonian power across most of the Fertile Crescent, from the Persian Gulf and the old Sumerian cities in the east, to the edge of mountains of Asia Minor and the borders of Syria in the west. Conquest was undertaken to secure essential supplies by the control of trade routes, and the exaction of tribute. Carvings show endless lines of conquered people bearing products to swell the stores of the great king, and the riches of Babylon became famous throughout the region.

Hammurabi was an absolute ruler, but he was anxious that his subject should know the laws under which

21

they had to order their lives. He therefore set up pillars in the temples on which were engraved all the laws which governed his kingdom, so that his subjects would be able to come and refer to them. This Code of Hammurabi was the first statement of the principle of 'An eye for an eye'.

Astrology played a vital role in all decision taking, and this led to Babylonians to study the stars closely. By 1000 BC their astrologers had plotted the paths of the sun and the planets with great accuracy, and they were able to predict eclipses. They instituted the system under which the circle is divided into 360 degrees and the hour into 60 minutes.

The first great period of Babylonian power ended when the city was destroyed by the Hittites in 1600 BC After that, Babylon remained an important centre of trade and culture, but a thousand years would pass before the city would achieve a late flowering of political power, under the great king Nebuchadnezzar.

The Hittites, who destroyed the first Babylon, were an Indo-European people, who had come into the area from the north, probably through the Balkans. After defeating Babylon, they dominated an even larger empire than that of Hammurabi, across the sweep of the fertile crescent, from their homeland in Anatolia, Asia Minor to the Persian Gulf and the borders of Egypt. The power of the Hittites was based on skill with iron. It was they who carried iron technology across the region.

Hittite power collapsed in its turn under pressure from the 'People of the Sea', who were also harassing Egypt at the same time. These People of the Sea, however, did not follow up their successes by founding an empire. Rather, they left a vacuum which was to be filled by the most terrible of the empires of the Ancient Near East.

Assyria. The centre of power now moved to the city of Nineveh on the middle reaches of the Tigris. Monuments of the great kings of Assyria, like Tiglath-Pileser I and Ashurbanipal show an empire based on brute military force and the use of terror to control conquered people. Whole populations, like the lost ten tribes of Israel, were moved from their homeland and resettled in other parts of the empire. In this way they lost the identity on which national resistance could be built.

Assyrian armies dominated the region from the 12th to the 7th centuries BC They marched north into the highlands of modern Turkey and Iran, looking for metals and other necessary supplies. They conquered Syria and Palestine, and, under Ashurbanipal in the mid 7th century, they even drove the Pharaohs of Egypt out of the Nile delta.

The Hebrews.

Among the Semite invaders into the Near East was a group known as the Hebrews. The Bible record tells how Abraham, the father of the people, left the city of Ur to return to a purer nomadic way of life. His descendants experienced a period of bondage in Egypt, from which they emerged in about 1300 BC.

The Hebrews made their home in Palestine, and they had set up a monarchy by about 1000 BC. Hebrew power reached its peak under King Solomon, who died in 935 BC The kingdom then split; Israel, the northern kingdom, was destroyed by Assyria in 722 BC and Judah, the southern, by Babylon in 587 BC.

The Hebrews do not feature in world history by virtue of their political success, but because of their religious faith. They proclaimed a single deity who they called Yahweh. The sacred writings of the Hebrews have been one of the major influences on the subsequent history of the world. Some themes need, therefore, to be identified.

Monotheism. Initially Yahweh was seen as the God of the Hebrews, who was set over against the gods of other peoples of the area. In time, however, Yahweh began to develop a uniqueness which challenged the existence of other gods. A writer from the period of the Babylonian exile pronounced Yahweh to be the god of the non-Hebrew, as well as the Hebrew people.

Divine Law. The rulers of Babylon and Assyria were absolute monarchs, whose word was law, and whose actions therefore could not be judged by any superior authority. The Hebrew prophetic tradition, in contrast, made it clear that a king, no less than any other person, operated under a divine law. Here, a ruler, who has unjustly taken a common man's vineyard, can be challenged by a prophet with the words 'Thou art the man!'

Man and Nature. The Hebrew creation myth, which was handed down verbally for many centuries before being written into the Book of Genesis, clearly sets man apart from the rest of creation. He is made in the image of God and given dominion over the beasts. The Bible has been the vehicle which has transmitted this perspective into Western culture.

Male Centred Religion. The Old Testament narrative describes the fierce rejection of female fertility gods of the Fertile Crescent, which the Hebrews described as The Abomination of Desolation. For the Hebrews divinity was uncompromisingly male, and woman is depicted as a secondary creation, born out of man's side. This rejection of the female strand of religion would later be modified in Catholic Christianity in the cult of the Virgin, but it has been influential in defining western attitudes on the relationship of the sexes.

Persia.

In about the year 1000 Aryan people moved south into the land which is now Iran (the land of the Aryans). There were two dominant tribes; the Medes occupied the north of the country, while the Persians occupied the south.

In the early centuries the Medish tribes were subject to the Assyrians, but they rebelled against their masters, and in 612 BC Nineveh was sacked and the Assyrian Empire was destroyed by the army of the Medes. The success of the Medes, as of the Persians after them, was based on their successful harnessing of the horse as an instrument of war.

The power centre shifted south when the Persian King Cyrus united Medes and Persians to form what was to become the greatest empire of the Near East. At its height, it extended from Greece and North Africa in the west to the Indus valley and the edge of the Central Asian steppe in the east. Darius the Great had problems at either edge of the empire – with Greeks in the west and Scythians in the east, but the bulk of the empire held together well until 330 BC.

The official Persian religion was Zoroastrianism. This emphasised the struggle of good and evil, and was to give the Semites the concept of angels and hell fire. It did not, however, seek converts, and the people of the empire were left in peace with their own gods. Cyrus was greeted by the Jews as the instrument of Jahweh, and he even rebuilt King Solomon's temple.

Darius was not as successful a conqueror as Cyrus, but he was an administrator of genius. Once a region had been brought within the empire, the royal satrap worked to win the trust and loyalty of the conquered people. Regional traditions were respected and local people were given responsibility in managing their own affairs. The country was bound together by roads, which could be used for trade and even postal services, as well as for armies.

India.

At its peak, the Persian Empire reached as far as the Indus valley. This was the home of another, distinct Asian civilization.

The Harappa Culture. Remains have been found in the Indus Valley of cities, dating from about 2550 BC. The pictogram writing of these early Harappa people has not been deciphered, but archaeologists have discovered houses, with bathrooms, built of burnt brick. There are remains of canals and docks, and Indian products from this period have been excavated in Mesopotamia. Rice was grown, which may indicate that the cities had contact with the Far East. Here is the first evidence of cultivated cotton.

The Harappan cities had houses, granaries and temples, but no palaces. This suggests that the civilization was centred around the priests, rather than around warrior kings. They were therefore probably ill equipped to meet the challenge of invaders.

The Aryans. In about 1750 BC Indo-European Aryans began to penetrate into the land from the north. They herded the cattle, which were to become sacred creatures. Their religion is enshrined in the oldest holy books of the world, known as the Vedas. From these it is possible to get an image of nomadic people, standing round their camp fire at night, chanting hymns to the sun and other forces of nature.

The Aryans overran the northern part of the continent, but they did not completely destroy the people who had been there before them. They slowly spread from the Indus, clearing the dense forest of the Ganges Valley and founding cities, such as Benares.

Hindu Castes. The racial structure of Aryan and non-Aryan people became enshrined in the caste system of India. There were three 'twice born' castes, which are assumed to originate from the Aryan invaders. The *Brahmins*, were the priests, the *Ksahiyas*, were warriors and the *Varsyas*, were farmers and merchants. Only members of these castes were permitted to take part in the Vedic rituals.

The *Sudras*, who came below the lowest member of the twice-born castes accommodated the conquered people. Below them were the unclean *outcasts*, who did not enjoy any caste status.

The Cults. As time passed, people looked for religious expressions which could engage the emotions

28

more fully than the Vedic hymns. The cults surrounding the gods *Vishnu* and *Shiva*, with their consorts, fulfilled their needs. It appears that Shiva, at least, was drawn from older pre-Aryan India. The cult of Shiva, who represented the great cycle of birth and death, life and destruction, was to express the Hindu world view most completely.

Buddhism. In the early 6th century BC a prince of the warrior caste, called Siddartha Buddha, left his home to seek enlightenment. He first followed the strict Hindu practices of fasting, but he did not achieve his objective. In the end he found that true enlightenment could only be discovered by 'letting go' of his own self, and accepting that, in life, all things are change. The Buddha rejected the caste system and his teachings took his followers out of Hinduism.

Although Hinduism and Buddhism separated, any contest for supremacy lay in the mind, for there were no wars of religion, like those which were to mark the West. The two religions share the same root. Both see man as an integral part of the natural world, not as a creature set apart from, and above it, as in the Hebrew tradition.

Buddhism received a great impetus with the conversion of the north Indian king Ashoka in 260 BC. He abandoned his career of conquest and administered his kingdom in the light of the teaching, providing the people with social works and good laws. In the end, Hinduism was to retain its hold on the sub-continent, apart from Ceylon in the south and the mountains of Tibet in the north, while Buddhism made its impact further east.

Central Asia.

Across the Himalayas from India lay the great land mass of central Asia. This can be divided into three bands. Furthest north was the great wall of the forests of Siberia. The centre consists of the Asian grasslands. In the south are the deserts and mountains. The last two are influential in world history from the earliest times until about 1500 AD.

In the grasslands of the steppe lived a selection of nomadic tribes. They survived in marginal land, much as, in later times, the Plains Indians would survive on the American prairie. The nomadic life could take peoples right across the grasslands, and they often fought each other for the control of land. Because the plain could only support a small population, drought, war or other impulses could set whole peoples on the move. This would produce a knock-on effect. Ripples could grow to waves. These would then break onto the boundaries of the lands which bordered onto the steppes.

These were illiterate people, so their names and history is confused, but they appear in history as the Hsiung-nu or Huns, the Avars, the Scythians, the Turks and the Mongols. They were terrible foes, who won their battles by great mobility and superb mastery of the horse.

Further south, in the desert region, lay the trade routes. From very early times Bactrian camels and horses carried goods along these trade routes, creating a link between Europe and the Near East to the west and China to the east. Most of the goods moved from east to west. At an early date, the Chinese learnt to make fine fabric from the web of the silk worm. Pepper and other spices also made light and high value loads. It was an immense and dangerous journey, but the profits were incentive enough to keep the caravans moving.

China.

Isolation and Contact. the people of China have long known of their nation as *Chung-hua,* the Central Nation. Educated people knew well of the existence of other cultures, but they were looked on as subordinate, and, indeed, tributaries of the great nation. Although the Chinese did maintain contact with the outside world, they were little influenced by it. Chinese culture was therefore able to establish a structure in the early centuries, which remained little altered throughout history.

The immediate concern of Chinese rulers, again from very early times, was to defend the northern borders against the steppe nomads. This border, which would be marked by the world's greatest building work, The Great Wall, lay along the line where the decline in rainfall made settled agriculture impracticable.

Culture and Language. The huge country centred on three rivers, the Hwang-Ho, the Yangtse and the Hsi. They were divided by great mountain ridges. A wide range of climates could be found within the nation. China has been politically divided for long periods, but she has maintained a unity of culture, beyond that achieved by any other people. An important reason for this is that, while the people of the west came to use to a phonic script, China retained the use of pictograms. The difference is fundamental. A phonic script is easily learned, but it needs to reflect the sounds of a language. People of different languages are therefore unable to communicate with each other without learning each other's language. This is inevitably culturally divisive. A pictogram script, in contrast, is hard to learn, but it is not linked to the sound of language. It can therefore be used to bind people who speak differently. China therefore developed a power to absorb and civilize the conquerors who, from time to time, spilled over her frontiers.

Literacy was the property of a cultured elite, whose whole education had, of necessity, been centred on diligence rather than creativity. This gave Chinese culture the twin characteristics of breadth and stability.

The State. Around 1700 BC the first historical dynasty, the Shang, gained control of the northern Hwang-Ho river valley. Even a this early stage, the court had archivists and scribes. Like their successors of later dynasties, the kings saw themselves as the bringers of civilization to barbarian peoples.

About 1100 BC the Shang were overthrown by the Chou who carried royal power to the central Yangtse river valley. Then, around 700 BC, the Chou in their turn were overthrown by pastoralists from the north. This brought in the time graphically known as the Period of the Warring States.

Confucianism. During this period there lived K'ung-fu-tsu, who became known to the world as Confucius. He looked back from that period of unrest to an earlier time when the world was at peace and believed that the problems of his times arose from the fact that people had forgotten their proper duty. In an ordered world, everyone had a place in society. Some – rulers, parents, husbands – were 'higher'; others – subjects, children, wives – were 'lower'. Everyone, high and low, was bound together in ties of mutual duty and respect. The high had no more right to oppress the low than the low had to be disrespectful of the high. When these bonds were broken, the times became out of joint.

Confucianism therefore placed emphasis on 'conservative' institutions – the state, the civil service, scholarship, and, above all, the family. It was not a religion, in the sense of teaching about God, but it brought a religious dimension to the worship of ancestors.

Social Structure. K'ung-fu-tsu accepted the most fundamental division in Chinese society. The common peasants were not allowed to belong to a clan, and they therefore had no ancestors to worship. Their lives consisted of an endless round of toil.

For those who were, more fortunately, born into a clan, China would become a land of opportunity. Even boys from poor homes could study to pass the necessary examinations, which would open up the coveted civil service jobs. For those with more modest aspirations, growing cities offered opportunities in trade and the crafts.

The fortunate lived in an assurance that Chinese customs and the Chinese way offered the model of excellence, and all other people had to be judged according to the way in which they measured up to this standard.

2. Mediterranean Civilization.

Early Sea-going People.

Conquering the Oceans. The earliest civilizations centred around major river valleys. The rivers provided water and arteries of communication. Then the technology of sails and ship building improved to a level which enabled men to venture onto the oceans. From early times, the Red Sea and the Persian Gulf provided important communication routes, which were orientated towards the east. The Mediterranean, particularly in winter, is subject to violent storms. Further advances in marine engineering, such as the construction of watertight holds and improvements in sails and rigging, were needed before sailors could master this environment.

By about 500 BC ships were able to move freely in the Mediterranean, at least in summer, so providing easier communication than was possible on land. There was then no distinction between a fertile north and an arid north shore. The whole region was fertile. Traders and rulers therefore saw the Mediterranean basin as a single unit, bound together by its ocean highway.

Minoa and Mycenae. In about 1900 BC a civilization grew up on Crete, which has been named after its King Minos. Its earliest writing has not been deciphered, but excavations reveal fine palaces and developed communities. Their cities stood beside the sea, and the builders were already confident enough in the control of their ships over the eastern Mediterranean to dispense with fortifications.

Objects found in Crete and Egypt show that there was a lively trade between the two cultures. The Minoan sailors probably traded in timber, wood, olive oil and grapes over the whole of the Mediterranean area.

Inhabitants of the Minoan cities were the first people to enjoy the benefits of piped drains and sewers, and wall paintings show them dancing and playing sports, including the Minoan speciality of bull leaping.

The Minoans set up colonies on the mainland, of which the most important seems to have been at Mycenae. This is the name which is given to Minoan civilization as it is found on the mainland. The culture spread across the Aegean to the coast of Asia Minor and to the city of Troy at the mouth of the Bosphorus.

The first Minoan civilization was destroyed by Indo-European people who poured into the region from the north. Some of these invaders settled in the Ionian peninsula to become Greeks. A later resurgence of Minoan civilization is thought to have been under Greek influence.

The stories which were written down centuries later by the poet Homer tell of the struggles between the Mycenaens of Troy and the less advanced Indo-European invaders.

The Phoenicians. Semite people, in general, liked to keep their feet on dry land. The exception were the people who lived in the area known as Phoenicia, which is now Lebanon and southern Syria. They developed remarkable skills as sailors and for centuries their ships dominated the trade routes. Phoenician sailors reached the Atlantic Ocean and traded with tin miners in distant Cornwall. The Greek historian Herodings even reports that one expedition rounded the southern cape of Africa.

The Phoenicians planted colonies to protect their trade routes. Most important, in about 800 BC they founded the city of Carthage. The colony was strategically placed to protect the ships which brought metal from Western Europe.

Phoenicia was never a power on land and, when, in 868 BC the Assyrian king 'washed his weapons in the Mediterranean' Phoenicia lost its independence. But the rulers of the great empires needed these fine sailors, and the Phoenicians therefore exercised influence beyond their military power.

Phoenicia is best known for its sailors. It did, however, make another major contribution to western culture, by creating a phonic alphabet. The words Alpha, Beta

37

and Gama are derived from the Phoenician words for an ox, a house and a camel.

The Greeks.

In Mycenaean times, an iron-working Aryan people were moving south into the Greek peninsula. Myths of early battles with Mycenaean Troy are preserved in the works of the story teller – or tellers – given the name of Homer.

The early culture was oral, but, in around 750 BC the Greeks adopted and modified the Phoenician alphabet and committed the ancient legends to writing. These were to provide the starting point for the world's first great literary culture.

The beginning of Greek civilization was dated from the first Olympian Games, held in 776 BC. This event, held once every four years, drew together people who shared the Greek language and culture. The participants did not, however, come under one unified government.

Government. The Greek political structure was dictated by the geography of the region in which they settled. This was a land of mountain ranges, with small coastal plains, which faced outwards to the sea. Each of these plains was settled by a self-governing community, which initially contained only as many people as the land would support. This was the basis of the *polis*, or city state.

The Iliad provides a picture of an early feudal society of kings, nobles and common fighting men. Each city then followed its own course in working out the structure of government. The first struggle lay between the kings (monarchy) and the nobles (aristocracy). Then pressure came from other influential citizens (oligarchy) and from the general mass of free male citizens (democracy). When a state plunged into chaos, a strong man (tyranny), who was often benevolent and public spirited, would emerge to bring order to the polis.

The Greek concept of democracy was specific to the confined structure of the city state. It did not operate through representative institutions, but through the direct participation of citizens in the decision taking process. The meeting place, or *agora*, not the temple or the royal palace, was now the centre of city life. The citizens who met here provided the city with its law courts and its political assembly. Debate and persuasion became vital skills. People could on occasion be swept away by the power of a demagogue, but within this forum they learned to listen and to analyse argument.

The fractured nature of Greek society did not provide peace and stability. The city states might join together in games, but they were as often at war with each other. For both good and ill, the people remained fiercely independent, more ready than any other people before, and perhaps even since, to question the structure of the

39

society within which they lived. *Colonization*. Since geography prevented expansion inland, the Greeks had an impetus to expand outwards, along the sea routes. Greek communities were established along the west and south coasts of Asia Minor, on the islands of the Aegean and as far east as Cyprus and westwards to Sicily and southern Italy, and even further into North Africa, France and Spain. These colonies were self governing, but they often had links with powerful city states, such as Corinth or Athens. They served both as an overspill for excess population and also as trading bases across the Mediterranean Sea.

The Persian Wars. the conflict between Greece and Persia has been depicted as a struggle between an oppressive empire and a freedom loving people. Reality is more complex. Close links had long existed between the Greeks and the Persians and many Greeks served within the Persian army. The trouble started when Greek city states in Asia Minor rebelled against Persian rule and Darius moved to put down the insurrection. The Asians were supported by the European Greeks, and this brought the Persian Empire into conflict with an alliance of Greek cities, led by Athens and Sparta. The army of Darius was defeated at Marathon in 490 BC and the navy led by his successor Xerses failed ten years later at Salamis. This war drew the boundary of the Persian Empire to the east of the area of Greek settlement.

Athens and Sparta. The alliance which had defeated Persia did not survive the victory. Athens was much the largest of the city states, with a larger population than its farm land could support. Prosperity was based on the control of silver mines, which were worked by thousands of slaves. The city's very survival therefore depended on a structure of trade and colonies. Whatever freedom may have been enjoyed by Athenian citizens within their city, their rule of others was often oppressive. The Athenians demanded heavy tribute from client states and put down rebellion as violently as any Persian army.

Other trading states, like Corinth, felt themselves continually threatened by Athenian power. They found allies in the conservative, agricultural state of Sparta. The Peloponnesian War lasted for 27 years, and ended with the defeat of Athens in 404 BC. This led to a reaction against an over-mighty Sparta, and the destructive sequence of wars continued into the 4th century. The Greeks may have provided the world with a vocabulary of politics and an ideal of democracy, but its outstanding achievement lies, not in politics, but in broader fields of culture.

Religion. Greek myth is drawn from the common Indo-European root, which created the Vedas in India. It has provided a fertile source of inspiration for western art and literature for more than 2000 years, but it is harder to look back through the twin filters of Semitic religion and

41

rationalism, which have shaped modern attitudes, to understand what the world of gods meant to the Greeks themselves. On the one side, there was a piety of the common man, which condemned Socrates for blaspheming against the gods; on the other side was a free thinking strain, expressed by the philosopher of 7th century Miletus, who declared 'If an ox could paint a picture, its god would look like an ox'. The Greek religious tradition was real, but it was not an all-demanding way of life, like that of the Hebrews.

Philosophy and Science. The Greeks invented organized abstract thought and took it to a level which would dominate the philosophy of the Near East and Europe until very recent times. In the Greek perspective, there was no distinction between the arts, the sciences, and, indeed, religion. All were a part of the search for truth. In the 6th century, Pythagoras did not distinguish mathematics from philosophy and religion. The two greatest Greek thinkers defined the twin, often opposing, channels through which all philosophy, and later, all theology, would flow.

Plato, a pupil of Socrates, was 23 years old when his home city of Athens was defeated by Sparta. His attempt to achieve a mental order was therefore born of the political disorder of the post war years. Plato is the apostle of the *ideal* – the abstract of perfection, whether it be for the state, the individual, or in a mathematical

42

equation. In his philosophy, all life is a striving towards an ideal of the good, containing truth, justice and beauty, which was the only reality in an imperfect world. Plato's Academy can lay claim to being the world's first university.

Aristotle came to Plato's Academy at the age of 17 and remained his master's devoted disciple. His interests, however, took him in the opposite direction, as he came to emphasize enquiry and experiment as the source of knowledge. While Plato stressed the *ideal*, Aristotle stressed the *real*; while Plato was drawn into the abstractions of mathematics, Aristotle found himself fascinated by the complexities of biology and literary criticism. For him, truth lay not in a distant abstract, but in a 'happy medium.' Aristotle is therefore seen as the father of the scientific method.

The Arts. 5th-century Athens provided the most fertile environment for classical Greek culture. The architecture of the Parthenon, the sculptures of Praxiteles and Pheidias provide an illustration in stone of the Platonic ideal. They provided generations of architects and artists, particularly from Europe, with a standard of perfection. Literature also flourished. Aeschylus, Sophocles and Euripides used the ancient myths to explore depths of the human experience and create tragic drama, while the irreverent Aristophanes, pioneered the tradition of comedy. The disasters of the Peloponnesian

43

Wars also inspired Thucydides to become the world's first scientific and literary historian.

The contribution of Greece to the world's cultural store is a fundamental theme of history. By the middle of the 4th century, however, the advances were largely confined to the Greek speaking world. The diffusion of Greek culture into a wider world would be the work of a young and brilliant student of Aristotle.

The Hellenistic World.

Alexander the Great. The state of Macedon lay to the north of Greece. It crossed the boundary which divided the civilized world from the barbarians. Philip II of Macedon developed his army into an efficient fighting machine and conquered the Greek city states. Philip died in 336 BC and was succeeded by Aristotle's pupil, his son, Alexander.

Alexander inherited his father's army, and the Greek power base. The problem he faced was how he could pay the soldiers who had served Macedon so well. This search for money took Alexander the Great on spectacular campaigns. There was ample booty to be won across the Aegean in the Persian Empire. In 334 BC the Macedonian army defeated the Persians at Issus. The army then marched south into Egypt, where Alexander founded the city which was to carry his name. He returned north, defeated the Persians once more and sacked the capital of

Persepolis. Not content, he took his army eastward into Afghanistan and the Punjab. He would have gone further, but his soldiers insisted that the time and come to turn back.

The young man was one of the great soldiers of all time. The importance of his conquests, however, was that they were the catalyst which brought together the old civilizations of the Near East and the newer Greek culture. Alexander was Greek, but he was drawn to Eastern ways. He himself married the Persian emperor's daughter, and, in a great symbolic gesture, he married 9000 of his soldiers to eastern women.

The Division of the Empire. Alexander died in Babylon in 323 BC at the age of 32, leaving no heir to succeed to his enormous empire. The land was divided between of his generals. The Ptolemies based their power in Egypt, the Seleucids in the region of Syria and the Attalids around Pergamum. Parthia later became independent of the Seleuchids. These were centralized states, under absolute monarchs. The age of debate and democracy was certainly past. Over most of the Hellenistic world, this was a time of economic growth, but the Greek cities themselves declined.

Hellenistic Culture. Greek was now the official and commercial language of the whole area. The learning of the scholars became widely known and great libraries were set up at Alexandria and Pergamum. Among the books preserved were many of the writings of Plato and Aristotle. Scholars in the Greek tradition worked in different parts of the Hellenistic world. Science flourished, as it would not do again for over 1500 years. In Alexandria Euclid laid the foundation of geometry. Aristarchus correctly deduced the structure of the solar system 1800 years before Copernicus and Eratosthenes measured the circumference of the earth. Archimedes of Syracuse had the widest ranging genius of all.

Philosophers, such as the stoics, could no longer question the ways of government, so they turned their thoughts towards the inner life of man. They led a quest for virtue and true contentment. Classical Greek styles provided powerful models for painters and sculptors, but Hellenistic artists retreated from the Platonic search for an ideal and worked instead to project the humanity of their subjects.

Religion. Greek religion was too restricted a vehicle for this new, expansive world. Mystery cults began to spread which demanded a more active devotion from their followers. Two of these became increasingly dominant. From Egypt came the myth of Isis and Osiris. This told of a dying and a rising god. From Zoroastrianism came the mystery of Mithras, with its powerful image of redemption through blood.

The End of the Hellenistic World. The Hellenistic empires in their turn fell to a new power from further west in the Mediterranean. The Roman victory at Actium in 31 BC marked the end of the era. No battle, however, could put an end to Greek culture. The Roman poet Horace summed it up by saying that, although Greece was defeated, it took its conquerors prisoner.

Republican Rome.

The Etruscans. In the years before 509 BC central Italy was dominated by a people called the Etruscans. They can be seen in lifelike tomb sculptures, but little is still known about their culture. They appear to have been an Indo-European people, who achieved dominance over other people by bringing iron working to a high level of perfection. Etruscan kings, the Tarquins, ruled in Rome until they were expelled, according to tradition in 509 BC. The expulsion of the kings remained a powerful myth within the Roman state. Men looked back to the days of the Tarquins as the time when the rights of the citizen were subjected to the will of a single individual.

The Structure of the State. The new Roman state was based on agriculture. Indeed, *pecunia*, the name for a flock or herd of animals, became the Latin word for money.

There were different groups within society. The old families who took pride in their status as *patricians*, assumed power in place of the deposed kings. The remaining free people were known as the *plebs*. At first

47

they were poor farmers, with little say in affairs of state. As Rome grew, however, many plebeians became more wealthy and they began to look for a share in the running of affairs.

Romans, be they patricians or plebs, took immense pride in their status as citizens. Roman citizenship became a unique badge of belonging to a pure and strong society, free from 'the softness and corruption of the Hellenistic world around them. Every man was liable to military service which could be for as long as 16 years in the infantry or 10 years in the cavalry. Warlike virtues were admired by society and inculcated in boys through the home and education. At best, this could breed a self-sacrifice to the common good; at worst it could bring a lust for battle and bloodshed.

The organization of the Roman Republic was not unlike that of a Greek polis. The Roman forum took the place of the Greek agora. The senate, which was an assembly of patricians, wielded the real power. Two consuls, elected from its ranks, commanded the army in war and were responsible for government in time of peace. The demand of the plebs to be represented was met by the appointment of two tribunes. It therefore became possible for an unusually talented man, from a low family, to rise in the state. This structure lasted for 450 years. It carried Rome from being a small city state to dominance in the Mediterranean basin.

Early Expansion. In the early centuries, Roman armies were occupied with winning control over the Italian peninsula. If there was a ruthless character to Roman expansion, there could also be generosity in the terms given on surrender. Conquered people were given Roman citizenship and allowed a large measure of self-government. Once within Roman rule, they too were expected to provide troops for the army.

The Punic Wars. As Rome expanded, she had only one serious rival. Carthage had expanded beyond North Africa. Her ships controlled the sea and Carthaginian colonies were established in Sicily, Southern Italy and Spain. The two powers were bound to clash for supremacy in the western Mediterranean. The Romans built up a navy, and in the First Punic War (264 – 241 BC) they defeated the Carthaginians at sea and won Sicily.

The Second Punic War (218 – 201 BC) marked the decisive struggle between the two powers. When Hannibal crossed the Alps and defeated Roman armies at Lake Trasimene and Cannae, it seemed as though Roman power would be broken. In 202, however, Hannibal was in turn defeated at Zama and Carthaginian power was destroyed. In 149 BC Rome took an excuse to fight a third Punic War. This time Carthage was flattened and the ground on which the city had stood was ploughed over.

The Rise of the Generals. Victory over Carthage had been bought at a high cost, and that cost was paid by the poor. Many peasant farmers, who were citizens, sold their land to the rich and so lost their means of support. This led to a period of internal unrest.

Wars were now being fought far from home, in the Hellenistic east and to the north in the land they called Gaul. Roads were built across the empire, which enabled the army legions to move swiftly from one trouble spot to another. These distant armies could no longer be commanded by consuls, with a term of office of two years.

There therefore arose a new breed of professional generals. These men often became fabulously rich on the booty of war, and, with a loyal army at their back, they could pose a threat to the traditional institutions of the Republic. Marius made his name in Africa and Gaul, and then Sulla in the eastern Mediterranean. Julius Caesar was the most successful in this line of successful generals. In 49 BC he took an irrevocable step when he crossed the river Rubicon, which marked the boundary of Italy, and marched on Rome at the head of his army. By this action he started the chain of events, which led to his murder, and the founding of imperial Rome.

Christianity.

Origins. The early years of the Roman Empire were to see the beginnings of another of the great religions of the world. The Jewish people had maintained a stubborn refusal to dilute their religion to meet the demands of Hellenistic rulers. At the time of Jesus of Nazareth, sects like the Essenes and the Zealots maintained a resistance to Roman rule.

Jesus was a Jew, but he appears to have rejected the path of political resistance and taught instead a message of the relationship of the individual to God and other men, closer to the teaching of some later rabbis. The content of Jesus' teaching was indeed to be influential, but his significance lay not in what he said but in what his disciples declared him to be.

The share of responsibility for his execution can not be determined from the documents preserved, so it is unclear whether he was executed as a danger to the Roman state or as a critic of Jewish practice. Whichever it was, his disciples declared that they had witnessed his resurrection, and proclaimed that he was the Son of God. They picked up the words of the writer from the Babylonian exile and announced him as the saviour of the world, and not just of a chosen people. The holy books of the new religion were written down in the Greek language of the Hellenistic world, rather than in the more restricted Aramaic language which Jesus himself spoke.

Christianity and the Mysteries. Paul of Tarsus carried the message in a series of missionary journeys through the Greek speaking world. There he spoke the language of the popular mysteries – of redemption through blood and of a dying and rising god. With Christianity, however, it was different, he declared. While the mysteries were based in mere images, Christianity was rooted in historical fact.

Paul and other missionaries always sought to found a Christian cell, which they called an *ecclesia*, the word used for the meeting of the Greek polis. Hellenistic culture provided a language for the new religion; Rome provided a structure which enabled it to spread. Missionaries could make use of the Roman roads, and they were not likely to be molested by bandits on the way.

There was no doubting the enthusiasm of the converts, but, for a long time, an outsider would not have readily recognized a fundamental difference between this religion and the mysteries. Heresies, like Gnosticism and Manichaeism were pulling Christianity away from its Semitic roots into the maelstrom of Hellenistic religion. The Roman army generally favoured Mithras. A long path of persecution lay ahead before Christianity would emerge as the dominant religion of the region.

Imperial Rome.

The Emperor. At the battle of Actium in 31 BC, Julius Caesar's great-nephew, Octavian, brought Egypt into the empire and ended the years of civil war. Four years later he was given the title of Augustus and made consul for life. He was careful to preserve the honoured republican institutions, but the senate lapsed into impotence and all power now lay with him.

No rule of inheritance was ever established for the position of emperor. In the centuries which were to follow, incompetents would be matched by administrators and generals of ability, imbeciles by philosophers. Most emperors died violently. Succession first passed through the house of Caesar. During one century of good government, it became the practice for an emperor to adopt his successor. For long periods, however, power fell to the general who could command the largest army. But the mass of people would never see the emperor in person. For them, success or failure had to be judged on whether he was strong enough to prevent the huge empire from breaking into civil strife.

The practice of emperor worship was imported from the old Persian tradition. The act of reverence due to the god-ruler was the symbol which bound together the hugely diverse people who now lay under Roman rule. Pious Jews refused to perform this ritual, but this was recognized to be a part of their ancient tradition and it was generally overlooked. The refusal of Christians, who came from all parts and races, was looked upon as a serious threat to the unity of the empire.

Buildings. The great monuments of Rome date from the Imperial age. Augustus himself restored 82 temples, and boasted, 'I found Rome of brick and left it of marble'.

Aqueducts, arches and the huge Colosseum still stand as monuments to imperial glory. The Romans were content to copy Greek styles, to which they added impressive engineering skills.

The more prosperous built homes, such as have been preserved at Pompeii and excavated across the empire. Here they built for comfort, and artists, working in paint and mosaic, expressed a less pretentious view of life with humour and grace.

Natural frontiers. The Roman armies had now carried the empire across Europe, Asia and Africa, until it had ten thousand miles of land frontier. Beyond lay barbarians, ever willing to invade and plunder. The task of defence was made easier by natural boundaries – the African and Arabian deserts and the great rivers Rhine and Danube. This line of defence had two weak points, lying on either side of the Black Sea. In Asia the entrance to the steppes lay open across the land of the Parthians. In Europe generals were tempted to go beyond the Danube, across what is now Rumania to the Carpathian Mountains. Roman armies suffered heavy defeats in both of these sectors. Claudius also carried the empire across the natural frontier of the North Sea to Britain. The expedition was designed to bring the glory of conquest and to win control of fabled metal mines of the wild island.

The City of Rome. By imperial times, Rome had

grown to be a huge city. Since most of the work was done by slaves, much of the population was unemployed, and the citizens had become accustomed to a life style supported by tribute from conquered peoples. No emperor could contemplate unrest in Rome, so the citizens had to be fed and kept amused on the famous diet of bread and circuses. Entertainments were on a massive scale. The Circus Maximus alone seated 190,000 people. Claudius built the huge harbour at Ostia, where grain, wild beasts and slaves were constantly being unloaded to feed the stomachs and the jaded palates of the people. The city gave nothing back to its empire.

East and West. Gradually a distinction began to emerge between the eastern and the western parts of the empire. The West, centred on Rome itself, covered western Europe and the old Carthaginian lands of North Africa. The east included the old Hellenistic world of Greece, Asia Minor, the Near East and Egypt.

The eastern side of the empire had a better balance to life. It contained ancient cities, but none dominated the region. It was self-sufficient in grain, wood, oil, wine and other essentials, with a surplus to buy in metal from the west and luxuries from the east.

The western part of the empire was not an area of ancient civilization. Since Carthage had been flattened, it had no cities to balance metropolis of Rome, which constantly sucked in products, so upsetting the economic balance of the region.

In 285 the Emperor Diocletian appointed a co-Emperor to rule the western sector. There was now an Empire of the East and an Empire of the West. In 324 Constantine accepted the dominance of the east by taking his capital to his new city of Constantinople.

The Triumph of Christianity. By this time, Christianity had established itself as a growing force. Diocletian tried to stem the tide, but Constantine accepted the new faith. Emperor worship may now have ceased, but even a Christian emperor could not shed the concept that he was the fountain of religion. He declared himself to be the thirteenth apostle and sat as chairman of the Council of Nicea, which established Christian doctrine. This set a precedent for the control of the church by the state.

At about the same time a group of hermits came together in Egypt to form the first monastery in the Christian tradition. This was destined to grow into an influential movement, capable of confronting the ambitions of Christian rulers.

The Barbarian Invasions. The century after Constantine saw increasing pressure on the European frontier of the Western Empire. Far away in the east, the Huns were on the move, and this created pressure on western tribes. The Huns themselves erupted into Europe under Attila in 440, to be defeated at Troyes in 451, but ahead of them, as if a prow wave, came Goths, Ostrogoths,

Visigoths, Franks and Vandals.

The Romans found it difficult to defend the long land frontier and they recruited barbarians to strengthen the army. In 376 about 40,000 armed Visigoths were allowed across the frontier. Then in 410 the Goths sacked Rome. Vandals, who left their name for mindless destruction, crossed through Spain into North Africa and then returned for an even more destructive assault on the great city.

In northern Europe, Angles, Saxons and Jutes crossed the North Sea, first to ravage and then to settle in the British Isles. The Celtic inhabitants, no longer protected by Roman legions, were driven back to the highland area of the West, and into Ireland, where the Christian faith survived and flourished.

Byzantium.

Her Frontiers. With the ancient capital in barbarian hands, the Roman Empire can be said to have fallen. Those who lived in the Empire of the East, however, recognized no such catastrophe. In 483 Justinian succeeded in Constantinople, and he set about the task of winning back the lost western lands. His armies recovered North Africa, Italy and Southern Spain. It appeared for a time as though the Roman Empire was still a reality. His conquests, however, were ephemeral. From his time onwards, the Empire of the East was under continual pressure.

In the East, Persia was a power of consequence once again, and behind her the steppe nomads were ever menacing. In the south the empire faced growing Arab power. In the north, Slav people were pressing into the Balkans. The Emperor Heraclius led the Imperial armies in more successful campaigns, but the pressure was ever inwards towards what was to be the Byzantine heartland of Asia Minor, Greece, the Balkans and southern Italy.

Cultural Life. The people saw themselves as being direct inheritors of the old empire. Citizens of Constantinople still visited the bath houses; they still followed the chariot races with the passion of a modern football supporter. Justinian completed the work of centuries of Roman jurists by compiling the authoritative digest of Roman law.

Byzantium, however, soon developed a distinctive character which set it apart from the old empire. This drew both from the Greco-Roman and from Eastern traditions. Constantinople remained a home of classical scholarship. Plato was particularly popular, but his thinking became overlaid by layers of mysticism. Classical features were used in buildings, but the great dome which rose over Justinian's Church of the Holy Wisdom demonstrated new skills and a new aesthetic. Secular artists still worked within Hellenistic traditions, but religious artists, in paintings and mosaics, were beginning to express a particularly eastern Christian piety.

Religion. The eastern church early developed a distinction between secular (living in the world) and religious (living out of the world) clergy. Secular clergy worked at the parish level and were allowed to marry. The ideal was set by the many hermits and monks who expressed their piety in extreme self sacrifice. Religious icons became the focus of devotion for ordinary people.

The emperor maintained Constantine's position at the head of the church. Patriarchs, bishops and priests lay under his power. Emperors decided doctrine and mercilessly persecuted many of their subjects who held 'heretical' beliefs. .

In the centuries after Justinian, the eastern and the western churches drew gradually further apart. In the west, the Bishop of Rome claimed primacy and began to build a centralized structure. The church finally divided into western and eastern parts in the Great Schism of 1054. This was partly about authority, partly about abstruse issues of theology, but it mainly stemmed lack of understanding of each other's piety.

The Arabs.

Mecca. The desert land of the Arabian peninsula was inhabited by fierce and independent minded Semitic tribes people, who were known as Arabs. They led a nomadic life of great hardship. One trade route between the Mediterranean and the Indian Ocean went across this land, passing through Mecca. The city was also a centre for pilgrimage to the sacred stone or *kaba*. The citizens of Mecca jealously guarded the revenues of both the trade and the pilgrimage.

Early in the 7th century a merchant, called Mohammed, had a vision and started preaching the message 'There is no god but Allah'. He came into conflict with the citizens of Mecca, and in 622 he left the city to live in Medina. This is the date from which the Arab world numbers its calendar.

Islam. The prophet Mohammed had met Christians and Jews and read many of their books and the religion which he founded lies within the Semitic tradition. He preached one god, which for him, ruled out the Christian concept of the Trinity. The word 'Islam' means 'submission' for the duty of the Moslem is to submit to the will of the one god. He gave his followers the five duties – daily prayers, alms, fasting, the keeping of Friday as holy day, and the pilgrimage – but the message was one of great simplicity. Very quickly, the feuding tribes of the peninsula were given that sense of community, which has ever since been the distinguishing feature of Islam.

Mohammed taught his followers that Christians and Jews were 'people of the book'. They and their religion had, therefore to be treated with respect. Once they accepted Moslem rule, they might be taxed, but they should not be persecuted or converted by force.

The Arab Conquests. Once the Arabs were united, they started raiding towards the north in search of booty, into the lands controlled by Byzantium and Persia. Their invasions had startling and unexpected success. This was partly because the two empires had weakened one another by endless warfare. More important, however, was that taxation and religious persecution had made their governments deeply unpopular with ordinary people. To 'heretical' Christians, the tolerant Moslem invaders seemed greatly preferable to either emperor.

The Persian Empire collapsed and Byzantium was pressed ever further backwards. Jerusalem fell in 638. It seemed as though Constantinople itself would fall, but in 717 the Arab armies were driven back from the city walls. By this time the Arabs not only controlled the Near East, but also North Africa and the whole of Spain. Their armies were even crossing the Pyrenees into the plains of Europe. Here, however, they found themselves in an alien environment of cold weather and barbarous people, so they turned back towards the south. The Arab armies carried Islam over this wide empire. Many conquered people converted; indeed Christianity disappeared completely from its old stronghold in North Africa.

The ultimate authority within the Islamic world lay with the caliphs. In 750 the ruling Umayyad house was overthrown and the new Abbasid rulers moved the capital to Baghdad.

Arab Culture. The Arabs possessed a powerful poetic tradition before the time of Mohammed and Islamic culture was founded in literature. The Koran, with its religious message, and its classical language provided a powerful unifying bond for one of history's more stable empires. Since the depiction of the human form was forbidden, art developed as elaborate geometric pattern. As the centre of empire moved out of the Arabian peninsula to Baghdad, so eastern influences became increasingly powerful. The Arabic language remained, however, the cement of the Islamic world. Although local dialects might vary, scholars from all parts continued to use the pure language of the Koran.

The Moslems did not come as the destroyers of civilization. The men from the desert quickly absorbed the cultures which they conquered. Their scholars read the Greek philosophers, and united them with the astronomy, mathematics and medicine of the east, so serving as the main channel for the ancient learning in a troubled world. Moslem civilization reached one of its peaks in Spain, where the university of Cordova was a major centre of learning.

The eastern Mediterranean remained the centre of thriving trade. War might bring temporary disruption, but trading links with the East were never long severed. From India came spices, pepper and sugar; from China came porcelain and silks. The wealthy of Byzantium had an insatiable taste for luxury goods and the Arabs soon came to share these sophisticated tastes. Byzantium controlled the overland routes to China, which ended at the Black Sea ports. The Arabs controlled the sea routes by the Persian Gulf and the Red Sea to India, with links beyond to China and the Spice Isles.

Threats to Arab Civilization. In time, Byzantium ceased to be a threat to the Islamic Empire; indeed it seemed only a matter of time before Constantinople must fall. From the 11th century, for some 300 years, Arab civilization would be subjected to assaults by Christian crusaders from Europe (Chapter 3) and successive waves of nomadic invaders from the steppes of Asia (Chapter 4). The latter were by far the more threatening of the two, and it was they who finally brought the great days of Near Eastern civilization to an end.

3. The Formation of Europe.

Church and State.

The Papacy. In the year 590 a new Bishop of Rome
was elected who would later be known as Gregory the
Great. He was a Roman from a senatorial family, but, in
the chaos of his day, he had made the choice to become
a monk. For a devout Christian the monastic life seemed
to be the only safe course to heaven in a violent and
turbulent world. But Gregory saw that it was pointless to
live with regrets for past glories of Rome or hopes for
help from Byzantium. The church now had a mission to
the restless and threatening barbarian world. Gregory
selected monks as missionaries and sent them to bring
Christianity to the barbarian tribes. Best known of these
was Augustine of Canterbury. At the same time, missionaries from Ireland were moving south from Scotland into
England and northern Europe. The missionaries from
Rome, however, succeeded in linking the growing church
back to Rome.

For Gregory's successors the first priority was to
establish the primacy of the bishopric of Rome, or

papacy. Popes claimed that, since they stood in a direct line from St. Peter, they had inherited his 'power to bind and loose'. A pope could therefore control men's eternal destiny by the weapon of excommunication. In an extreme situation, he could even place an interdict, which forbade the performance of any sacraments, on a whole country. In an age of faith this was a formidable sanction.

The Popes had first to bring the Christian clergy under their control. Ordinary parish priests were generally illiterate peasants; bishops were temporal lords who used the church as a means of expanding family lands. Most were married men, who expected to pass their lands and livings on to their children. Their prime allegiance was therefore to the king or chief, rather than to a distant pope.

Monasticism. Only the monks were free from these temporal ties. The Rule of St. Benedict, which imposed poverty, chastity and obedience, was now widely accepted. The monks were also almost alone in being literate in an uncultured world. This meant that they could reach positions of influence in both church and state.

The popes used monks as their representatives, and, wherever possible, promoted them to high positions within the church. In time the popes worked to extend their control over the secular clergy by forbidding clerical marriage altogether.

A Time of Turbulence. In the early centuries after the fall of Rome, the pope and his monks were able to establish respect and authority because they provided the only apparent stability in a troubled society. Groups of barbarians roamed through Europe, bound to their leaders in simple tribal ties. When they settled down and adopted Christianity, much of the old way of life continued. Society still had no recognizable political structure, in the modern sense. Disputes were still settled by traditional 'rough justice', such as the ordeal and trial by battle.

Change continued slow in the dark forests of Germany. In time, however, the Franks and other groups in the western part of the European mainland adopted a form of Latin as their language, and paid some respect to the Roman legal system. The tribes who were more cut off in the British Isles, continued to speak their own German language, and developed law, based on past rulings, as preserved in the minds of the elders. So developed the divisions between the romance and Anglo-Saxon languages, and between Roman and common law which were to become important in later western civilization.

Political and social order was beginning to emerge by the end of the 8th century, but then Viking ships brought new danger to European coasts. It is never easy to say why a people go on the move, but it appears as though population growth and weather problems disturbed the balance of marginal Scandinavian farming. Certainly the feared Norsemen set off on 'land takings' and voyages of plunder. Their ships spread out across the North Atlantic to Iceland, Greenland and North America; they emerged into the Mediterranean; they sailed down the great rivers of central Asia, setting up the Russian state, and reaching Constantinople; they won control of northern Britain and Normandy. In 1066 a family of Norse descent won the crown of England.

The Norsemen were not the only raiders. Men from the steppes, this time the Magyars, were pillaging from the east and Moslem Saracen raiders came from the south. Hardly any part of Europe escaped. The unfortunate monks of Luxeil had their monastery burned by Norsemen, Hungarians and Saracens.

The Empire. For a brief period a new power arose in Europe. In 771 the ruthless and talented Charlemagne succeeded to the whole of the Frankish kingdom. For the next 40 years he led his armies to victories on all his borders, even mounting the first counter attack against Islam in Spain. Charlemagne was more than a conqueror. He was a devout Christian, and did much to spread the faith – by the sword if necessary – across Europe. He also respected learning, and he could read himself, although writing defeated him. He encouraged the clergy to respect books and learning, he founded schools and brought the best minds of the day to his court.

On Christmas Day, 800, he was crowned by Pope Leo III in the church of St Peter in Rome. The people cried, 'to Charles Augustus, crowned by God, great and peaceful Emperor of the Romans, Life and Victory.' A new Roman Empire had been proclaimed.

The empire was based on one man's will, and, like Alexander's, it fell apart on Charlemagne's death. It was divided into three parts. The central kingdom did not survive, but the two other halves would ultimately become France and Germany. Charlemagne's eastern successor retained the title of Holy Roman Emperor, but his lands remained a loose confederacy. In 940 the Comte de Paris, Hughes Capet, won the French crown and established a monarchy which was to survive until the French Revolution. His family was the first European dynasty to establish the concept of a hereditary monarchy.

Powers Temporal and Spiritual. After Pope Leo III had placed the crown on Charlemagne's head, he stretched himself on the ground as a sign of honour to the Emperor. Laster popes would regret this gesture. The first objective of the Popes was to win control within the church. This involved taking the right to appoint bishops away from the temporal rulers.

In the 11th century, Pope Gregory VII and Emperor Henry IV came into conflict in the Investiture Controversy. Gregory was victorious, forcing Henry to stand barefoot in the winter snow as a sign of submission. Gregory then formulated the extreme claim that all power came from the pope, and he therefore had the right to appoint and depose kings and emperors. The Investiture Controversy was the first of a series of disputes between church and state. They involved, not only the Holy Roman Emperor, but also kings of France and England.

King, Lord and Parliament.

The Feudal System. In those troubled times, people were prepared to sacrifice liberty in the interest of security. Kings and emperors were remote figures, so free men bound themselves to their local lord, who could give assistance when danger was near. When a man took an oath of loyalty he gave his lands to the lord, and then received them back as the lord's vassal. He had the obligation to follow the lord to war, but as a mounted knight, to set him apart from the common serfs. The lord, in his turn, bound himself to a higher lord, and the king stood at the apex of the pyramid. Only the serfs were nobody's vassal, because they had nothing to give in exchange for protection. These common people were not allowed to leave their villages, to go to school or to get married without their lord's permission.

By the end of the 9th century, this feudal system had

spread to all but the most remote areas of Europe. Kings, like other lords, were concerned to extend their lands wherever they could by war and dynastic marriage. The two way nature of the feudal compact served as a check on royal power. In France, the Capetian kings stood at the apex of the pyramid, but for long periods their actual power did not extend beyond their own lands around Paris. So, when the King of England married a French heiress, he did homage to the French king for his lands in Aquitaine, but he did not permit any interference within his territory.

The Hundred Years War between France and England was fought sporadically from 1337 to 1453. The English king may have laid claim to the crown of France, but it remained in essence a struggle between a dynastic monarch, determined to establish direct control over feudal lands on the one side, and an over mighty subject, on the other. It was one of the catalysts which defined the meaning of the modern nation state. Writing some 200 years later, Shakespeare would put words of nationalistic fervour into the mouths of John of Gaunt and Henry V. Such sentiments would have been incomprehensible in the time of Charlemagne or William the Conqueror, but they were beginning to have some meaning to their supposed speakers.

King and Parliament. William the Conqueror gave English kings more direct authority within their own realms. The feudal system was constructed to ensure that no lord could become 'over mighty'. Vassals, for their part were concerned that the king should not achieve unlimited power. In 1215 the lords forced King John to sign Magna Carta, which laid down two basic rights – that no free man could be imprisoned without a trial and the king could not raise taxes without the consent of a Great Council. In 1295, King Edward I called what became known as the Model Parliament, because it set the pattern for future parliaments. Representation was by estates – the Lords temporal, the Lords Spiritual and the Third Estate, with the first two sitting together in an upper house. It was also established that parliament had the responsibility to act as the highest court in the land, to give advice to the king, to make laws and to vote taxes.

The Rise of the Towns. The inclusion of the third estate in Edward's Model Parliament was testament to the growing importance of trade in the European economy. Wealth was no longer the preserve of landowners and the church, so, to achieve maximum income, it was now necessary to consult with the representatives of the growing towns.

As towns grew in importance, kings gave them charters, which assured them freedom from interference by local landowners. Their walls were the symbol of their independence, and magnificent churches the evidence of their wealth. Trade provided a means by which low born men could rise to positions of power within their own community, and even within the state. Different occupations were organized into guilds, which controlled terms of entry, quality standards and gave members a social structure.

The cities were often natural allies to kings who wanted to centralize power. Overmighty nobles might flourish in conditions of civil war, but merchants needed the peace, which only a strong government could provide. Kings, for their part, recognized that the growing wealth, which was the basis for national strength as well as royal revenue, was generated, not on noble estates, but inside the town walls.

The Cloth Trade. The Lord Chancellor of England, still sits in the House of Lords of a Woolsack. This was a reminder to parliament that the nation's wealth rested on the woollen trade. England, however, stood in the lowly position of a primary producer; the business in finished cloth centred round Flanders. Flemish weavers jealously guarded the trade secrets which made their cloth the most sought after in Europe. From the 13th century, the economy of northern Europe became increasingly sensitive to fluctuations in the fortunes of the cloth trade.

The Crusades.

The First Crusade. In 1095 the Byzantine emperor

appealed to the pope for assistance against the Turks. The pope answered the call by preaching a Holy War. The motives of those, both noble and common folk, who took the cross, were very mixed. Many of the Norman lords who took the lead saw the opportunity of a new land taking, like those of their Viking ancestors. But there was also a real devotion. The two were not incompatible. When the army arrived first in Byzantium and then in the Arab lands, they appeared like barbarians, with nothing to recommend them but their brute courage. Jerusalem fell to the crusaders, who waded through blood to give thanks for the victory.

Outremer. The crusaders established states in the conquered land. The Moslems resented these Christian enclaves in their territory and they were under constant pressure. In 1187 Saladin reconquered Jerusalem and the crusaders were unable to win it back. In 1291 the last Christian outpost fell to the army of Islam. The crusades gave the West two centuries of contact with a higher culture. Knights returned home with a taste for oriental luxury goods; some picked up an interest in learning and mathematics; methods of castle construction and siege warfare were modernized on Arab models.

The Later Crusades. Eight campaigns between the 11th and the 13th centuries are known as crusades, as well as tragic children's crusades. The movement turned inwards against European heretics. The simple crusaders were not always able to distinguish which enemy they should fight. The Venetians encouraged the fourth crusade to turn on Byzantium. In 1204 Constantinople was captured by the crusaders and the city remained in Christian hands until 1261. Although the rump of empire would survive into the 15th century, Byzantium never recovered from the disaster.

Spain. At the same time, Christian forces were counter-attacking against the Moslem Moors in Spain. In 1212 the Moors were defeated and driven back to Grenada. The reconquest of the peninsula was completed in 1492. A great culture was replaced by a fanatical Christian state, in which the Inquisition was used as a tool of persecution against Moors, Jews and many Christians whose views did not please the authorities.

Learning, Art and Society.

Scholarship and Authority. As long as there was no nation state, there were no sharply defined national boundaries. Latin provided a lingua franca and the church a broadly based structure within which the educated of their day could communicate.

Through the troubled times any learning remained behind monastic walls. The books of early Christian fathers were copied and became the intellectual authorities of the new world. Men had lost confidence in their own ability to reach conclusions, either through logic or through experiment, and all argument therefore referred back to authority. Even quite trivial issues of dispute would be decided by the weight of authority which could be mustered on the one side or the other.

The authors of antiquity were largely unknown until around the 12th century. Then translations began to be made into Latin from copies preserved in Islamic Spain and Sicily. The ancient dichotomy between Plato and Aristotle began to be reflected in arguments between nominalist and realist theologians. Thomas Aquinas, in particular, baptised Aristotle. This did not, however, lead to an increase in experiment; classical authors joined the Christian fathers as valid sources of authority. In southern Europe, men still lived amidst the ruins of classical civilization. The classical and the Christian came together until, as in Dante's Inferno and Michelangelo's Sistine Chapel, they became indistinguishable from each other.

By the 12th century, learning was coming out from monastic walls into the more open atmosphere of universities. The first to be opened was at Salerno, where Islamic and Byzantine influence was strong. Then came Bologna, Paris, Oxford and many others. Crowds would follow teachers, like Peter Abelard, who spoke a new and more restless language. Students at university were in religious orders of some sort, but the educational impetus continued outwards into the wider population. By later medieval times, an increasing number of lay people, particularly in the towns, were acquiring literacy.

Architecture and Painting. In early medieval times most stone buildings were either castles or monasteries. Many were fine buildings, but they added little to the techniques of antiquity. By the 12th century architects were developing their own signature. The Romanesque style of Southern Italy was based closely on a study of classical models. In northern France and England there rose magnificent cathedrals in the Gothic style. Here the pointed arch and the flying buttress enabled them to give their structures both height and light.

Most painting, likewise, remained dedicated to the church. Altar pieces showed the Virgin and child, with patrons and saints; frescoes and stained glass windows reminded illiterate worshippers of Bible stories; monks, copying psalters and books of hours, under no pressure of deadlines, painted exquisite decoration. In Italy, the school of Sienna worked under direct influence from Byzantium. But painters, like architects and stone masons, were craftsmen who were happy to work for any patron, and, as the centuries passed, an increasing number of commissions were available for secular work.

Literature. Medieval literature, like that of any other period, was made up of different strands – folk tales and myths, national histories, historical chronicles, love poems and works of devotion. Early vernacular literature, like Norse sagas and the Anglo-Saxon Beowolf, helped to create national language areas. In the early centuries, however, Latin was the language of both secular and religious writing.

By the 14th century a new vernacular literature was emerging. The supreme example of in English is *The Canterbury Tales*, written by soldier and customs officer, Geoffrey Chaucer, for an audience of other lay people.

Times of Change.

The Black Death. A sickness new to the human race was first reported in the Yangtze Valley in 1334 and, according to one estimate, some 13 million Chinese died in the following years. Relentlessly it spread from east to west, leaving devastation in India and across Asia. In 1347 the plague spread across Northern Italy and in the following years it is estimated that between a quarter and a third of the population of Europe perished. This first outbreak was the worst, but the disease returned periodically until the second half of the 17th century. Although it was a world wide phenomenon, its effects have been most closely studied in Europe.

Initially it brought economic collapse; prices of all goods fell sharply and much farm land returned to nature. As life recovered, employers were faced with an acute labour shortage. This created strains within the social structure of both town and country. Guild regulations were flouted and the feudal structure began to crumble. There were major peasant uprisings, in France in 1358, in Florence in 1378 and in England in 1381.

The Late Medieval Church. Pious Christians were unable to understand why God could have created such destruction. The plague accentuated a Christian piety which identified God as judge and destroyer and the saints, particularly the Virgin Mary, as protector.

The church, like all institutions, moves through cycles of corruption and reformation. In early medieval times, reformation came from within. The last of these reforming movements was the founding of the friars by Francis of Assisi in 1209. Now the impetus for reform had grown weak. In the 14th century popes taxed the faithful heavily to maintain a lavish lifestyle. After the Black Death these taxes fell all the more heavily on a smaller population. One fund raising technique was the offer of indulgences, by which punishment in the next world was remitted in exchange for payment in this world. During the 14th century the church lost its independence when it moved under the protection of the King of France in Avignon. The Great Schism, when rival popes competed from Rome and Avignon, further undermined spiritual authority. Some Franciscans denounced papal luxury and were burned as heretics but their message was heard by the people.

Before the end of the 14th century John Wyclif in England and Jan Hus in Bohemia were preaching that man did not need the apparatus of the church to make contact with God. Hus founded what was to be the first protestant church, and Wyclif translated the Bible into English.

The Reformation. In the early 16th century the pope set out to raise money for the building of St. Peter's by selling indulgences. In 1517, the university lecturer Martin Luther challenged the papal representative to a debate by nailing 95 theses to the door of Wittenberg cathedral. The church authorities sought to have him condemned, like heretics of old, but he found protection from German princes. The protestant movement soon won followers, particularly in the trading towns and in Northern Europe.

Luther did not initially see himself as the leader of a movement which would split the western church, but, as he preached the supremacy of the Bible and faith over the sacraments and traditional authority, the division quickly became irreconcilable. He found himself leading a mass movement, based on individual piety. Luther was the catalyst for another round in the ancient struggle between lay and secular powers. He only survived to preach because he was adopted by German princes, who saw his movement as a useful weapon against the power of the church.

Eastern Europe.

Russia. It appears as though the Norsemen who settled the rivers of Russia brought no women with them, so the process of assimilation was rapid. In 980 Vladimir established the kingdom of Kiev and he married a sister of the Byzantine emperor. It is said that Russian envoys visited Constantinople and the West to decide which form of Christianity should be adopted. They were overwhelmed by the splendour of Constantinople, and the eastern link was forged. Kiev was destroyed in 1169 and the centre of power was driven northwards to Moscow. Trading and cultural ties with Byzantium were largely lost, and Russia was increasingly isolated until it was overrun by the Mongols in the 13th century. Russian independence can then be dated to the victory over the Tartars in 1380. The Grand Princes of Moscow emerged as rulers and Ivan III (1462-1505) adopted the title of Tsar (Caesar) and the double headed eagle, to substantiate the claim that, with Constantinople in Ottoman hands, the Russian monarchy had now inherited the imperial tradition.

Poland. When Vladimir made his choice of the eastern church, the Poles on his western frontier had just turned in the other direction. The missionaries who brought western Christianity to Poland also acted as forerunners for waves of land-hungry German invaders, led by the fearsome Teutonic Knights. In late medieval times, a Polish state lay across the central European plain, with its prosperity based on grain exports to the west through the port of Danzig. It was, however, already showing signs of the damage that would be caused by its geographical location as a buffer between Western Europe, the Scandinavian north, Russia and the East and the disturbed cauldron of Slavs and Magyars in the Balkan south.

In both Russia and Poland the serfs lived in great poverty, under the control of a wealthy landed class. Rulers were faced with a perpetual challenge from overmighty subjects without being able to look for the support of any considerable middle class.

4. The Wider World.

Asia Before the Mongols.

India. For centuries after Ashoka, the Indian sub-continent was divided into warring states. The south, behind its mountain barrier, remained the home of non-Aryan people. They maintained contact with the Mediterranean civilizations through the Red Sea and Persian Gulf trading routes. In the north-west, the frontier and Indus valley remained open to Asian invaders. Invading Hunas, probably Huns, devastated this region, as they did lands both to east and west.

In about 320 AD the Guptas united the whole of northern India. This marked the great age of Hindu culture. In the 5th century, the decimal system was invented, so opening new areas of mathematics. Sculpture and literature flourished, both achieving a broad unity of style, characterized by a warm sensuality. Buddhist culture declined as Hinduism spread across Asia and into the islands of the Pacific. The island of Bali remains today a marker of this great expansion.

The Hindu Empire was in time challenged by the rise

of Islam. Moslem traders – always effective missionaries for the Prophet – would have visited the western ports in the 7th century. By the 8th century invaders were crossing the open north western frontier. By the 12th century, they controlled the Punjab and a century later they dominated the Ganges valley. The fateful religious divide was now established.

China. China was united more effectively by language and culture than it was by its political structure. The two most powerful dynasties were Han (c. 205 BC – 220 AD) and T'ang (618 – 907). Their empires were comparable to that of Rome at its most powerful. During the T'ang Dynasty trade flourished, and China became a major sea power, with trade reaching from the Persian Gulf in the west to Indonesia in the east. The great Chinese dynasties had an expectation of life of about 300 years. They were founded by a great individual who combined military and administrative skills. In later years, as the succession passed to lesser men, the state would come under pressure from nomads to the north and rebellion at home. Imperial authority was upheld by officials, who preserved the traditions of K'ung-fu-tsu. Their main tasks were to take the census and keep the land register up to date. Beyond that, they maintained only a broad supervision over local lords, who raised taxes and performed the day to day tasks of administration themselves.

Great civil works were undertaken. The country was now bound together by canals, most important of which was the Great Canal, which linked Peking with Hang-chou. Huge irrigation projects were undertaken to provide food for the ever growing population. The casting of iron, printing, the magnetic compass, the use of paper money and explosives were all pioneered in China, but the conservative structure of society militated against the fullest exploitation of her inventions.

In the periods between the great dynasties, the country relapsed into warring states. There were times of disaster, when armies ravaged large areas, but in general, conditions changed little for the mass of peasants, whose life was always more closely governed by local lords than by distant emperors. But, while Europe remained divided into her warring states, China could always be drawn together once again by a dynamic new dynasty.

The Sung Dynasty (960 – 1279) was never as powerful as its great predecessors and in 1127 it lost the northern part of the country to Chin invaders. In the following century and a half the Southern Sung Dynasty lacked military power, but the period is viewed by many as the high point of Chinese culture. The Imperial capital of Hang-chou was a centre of wealth, culture and leisured living, far beyond any other city in the world.

Sung art was influenced by the Zen school of Buddhism. Painters, such as Ma Yuan, worked with an economy of line and colour to make a visual statement about man's position within the world order. Potters made dishes which looked 'like ivory, but were as delicate as thin layers of ice'.

The Seljuk Turks. The name 'Turk' is given to widely dispersed people, originating on the Asian steppes, who spoke a common language. In the 10th century a chief called Seljuk settled with his people near Samarkand and was converted to Islam. The tribe organized an army based on slaves, mainly recruited from southern Russia and the Caucusus, who were known as mameluks. Backed by these fearless warriors, Seljuk's grandsons built an empire, from Azerbaijan and Armenia, into the ancient lands of Middle East. They overran Persia, captured Baghdad, Jerusalem and Egypt and invaded Byzantine lands in Asia Minor.

Later Seljuks rulers found it difficult to hold this vast empire together. While their efforts were largely directed against European crusades, they faced trouble in other parts of the empire. In Egypt, for instance, mameluke soldiers established a virtually independant government. The Seljuk Empire therefore became vulnerable to another and greater threat from the Asian steppes.

The Mongols.

Genghis Khan and his Successors. In 1206 a chief called Temujin, better known to the world as Genghis

Khan, united the Mongol tribes who lived in the area today called Mongolia. These were wild, nomadic peoples in the tradition of the horsemen who had come from the steppes throughout recorded history. He then established dominance over the more numerous Turkish peoples from the land to the north of the Himalayas. Genghis Khan came to believe that he was destined to rule the world, and he embarked on the greatest programme of conquest in history. His followers were magnificent horsemen. As a nomad people, they could survive on dried milk and the blood of their horses. Released from the constraints of supply, they were therefore uniquely mobile. They were also utterly ruthless. Cities which accepted them were often treated with leniency; those that resisted were liable to be levelled to the ground, and the population massacred. As the reputation of the Mongol horde was carried ahead, rulers capitulated to avoid the dreadful destruction.

By the time that Genghis died in 1227, the Chin Empire of northern China had fallen, and Mongol armies had swept across the open grasslands of Asia as far as Russia and the Caucasus. Still the advance continued. In 1237-8 the Russian state was overwhelmed by horsemen who rode down the frozen rivers, achieving the winter conquest which would later elude both Napoleon and Hitler. When a Great Khan died the armies returned to their homeland to debate the issue of succession. Europe might have been overrun had Genghis Khan's successor not died in 1241. The armies did not again threaten Europe; to the Mongols, it seemed a poor land, hardly worth conquering. They did, however, return to the Middle East, capturing Baghdad and destroying the caliphate in 1258. The tide of conquest finally turned here too when, in 1260, the mamelukes of Egypt organized the armies of Islam to defeat a Mongol army at Ain Jalut, near the town of Nazareth.

Mongol China. The Mongol Empire was now divided into four, with the eastern section the portion of Genghis' grandson, Kublai. He led a Mongol assault on the Southern Sung Empire, which fell in 1279. Further expeditions were launched into South East Asia and even, unsuccessfully, against Japan. While his grandfather Genghis had devastated the north, Kublai respected the civilization which he conquered. Although he spoke little Chinese, he was a patron of literature and, like conquerors before him, he adopted Chinese ways. Mongol rule had now united the whole territory between Europe and China under a single authority and the ancient overland routes were opened once again. In 1275 members of the Polo family from far away Venice reached the court of Kublai Khan. When the young Marco Polo finally returned to Venice in 1299 he gave the west its first information about the civilization of the east. Readers in the more primitive Europe found it hard to believe that such a land of riches could exist far to the east, but some two centuries later a Genoan sailor called Christopher Columbus would own and make notes on a copy of the Venetian's narrative.

For the Chinese, however, the Mongols remained a dynasty of foreigners. Prosperity declined sharply and there was a wave of unrest, and the Mongols were overthrown in 1367 by a new Ming Dynasty. This survived its allotted three centuries until in 1644 it was in turn overthrown by new invaders from Manchuria, who established the Manchu Dynasty.

Later Mongol Conquests. In about 1370 Timur the Lame, a chief from the region of Samarkand, proclaimed that he was the man to revive the Mongol Empire. In the next 30 years, he ravaged the Middle East, Asia Minor, Southern Russia and Northern India with a brutality only matched by his distant kinsman Genghis Khan. The ancient lands of the Fertile Crescent, so long the focus of world civilization, never recovered from his invasion. The Mongol Khanate of the Golden Hoarde in Russia was fatally weakened. He died in 1405, when on his way to carry his conquests into China.

In time the Mongol people of Central Asia and the Middle East came to accept the religion of Islam. The weakness in Mongol power lay in the fact that there was no established law of succession. Timur's successors, like other Mongols, were concerned with domestic issues as they contested succession. Fifth in line from Timur was the more attractive Babur. The kingdoms of northern India were at that time in a state of permanent warfare. In 1526 Babur won a series of victories, and by his death in 1530 he had established Mongol – or Mogul – rule in northern India.

Mogul India.

Akbar. In 1556 Babur's 14 year old grandson, called Akbar, inherited a weak and divided empire as a boy of 14. He also inherited the ancestral belief that no empire can survive unless it is continually expanding, and throughout his reign he kept his armies constantly on the offensive. He continued old mongol tactics. When a city, like Chittor, resisted it could be utterly destroyed and its people massacred; when people accepted his authority, they found him a generous ruler. By 1600 his Mogul Empire controlled the whole of the sub-continent, except for Ceylon and Vijayanagar in the south. Akbar built a huge capital at Fathpur-Siki, which was to be the model for Mogul public buildings of incomparable grandeur, culminating in Shah Jahan's Taj Mahal.

The country was divided into provinces, but all authority sprang directly from the Emperor himself. Although a ruthless conqueror, Akbar was anxious to bind his people together effectively, and he was concerned at the religious division which existed between his Hindu and Moslem subjects. He was suspicious of all dogmatism, and devout Moslems accused him of back-sliding when he abolished the poll tax payable by Hindus, and worked to find a compromise between the two religions.

The Decline of the Mogul Empire. Akbar was an outstanding ruler, but his empire suffered from weak-nesses inherited from his Mongol tradition. In Europe, structures of government were coming into existence which transcended the personality of the ruler. In Mogul India, however, authority continued to be over-depend-ant on the ability of one man. In his last years, even Akbar was plagued by rebellious sons. The instability of the empire can be illustrated from events at the end of the reign of Shah Jehan. In 1657 he fell ill, triggering a ferocious civil war between his sons. The victorious Aurangzeb was a devout and intolerant Moslem and under his rule the united empire created by Akbar began to fall apart.

The Ottomans.

The Foundation of Empire. Mongol successes in central Asia created more movement of nomad tribes out of the grasslands. In the late 13th century one Ertughrul led a band of followers, who were equally devoted to Islam and to plunder, into the Seljuk lands of the Middle East. Ertughrul's son, Othman overthrew the Seljuk sultans, and founded the great empire which was to bear his name.

Othman's successors defeated the Byzantine army. They captured Asia Minor, and, in 1361, crossed into Europe to establish Ottoman power in the Balkans. Constantinople was now an isolated fortress in Ottoman lands, and in 1453 it fell to the Sultan Mehmet II.

The Spread of Empire. Ottoman power reached its peak in the century after the fall of Constantinople. In the early 16th century Selim I marched southwards, defeating the Mamelukes of Egypt and capturing Mecca, where he was proclaimed Caliph of the Islamic world. His successor Suleiman I, the Magnificent, turned north. In 1526 he defeated the Hungarian army at the great battle of Mohacs. Three years later his armies laid siege to Vienna.

Africa.

Trans-Saharan Trade. Historians of early sub-Saharan Africa are restricted by the lack of written records and the destructive capacity of termites, working on wood and mud brick. The continent, however, was far from isolated. A thriving trade existed across the Sahara trade routes between North Africa and the grassland region which lies across the continent from near the Atlantic to the Nile.

The staple product being carried southward was salt

– an essential commodity for people living in a hot climate. The Moslem traders who crossed the desert carried various luxury goods, and also brought their religion and literacy in Arabic script. On the return journey they carried gold, slaves and leather goods. Before the time of Columbus, Europe was heavily dependant on African gold and 'Morocco leather' has always originated south of the Sahara. A key focal point of this trade was Timbuktu, on the Niger, which became famous as the meeting point of the camel and the canoe. The town was already well enough known to be marked on a Spanish map in the late 14th century.

The gold and probably most of the slaves came form the forest region still further south, so trade reached out in both directions. Among the most active traders were the Hausa people, who were based on city states, such as Kano, and Zaria. They would be late recruits to Islam and they never organized into larger political units.

African Empires. Broadly based political structures did, however, come into existence in the Southern Sudan to control the two-way trade. The Empire of Ghana (8th – 11th centuries), was succeeded by Mali (12th – 14th centuries) and Songhai (14th – 16th centuries). Kings like Musa Mensa, who ruled Mali in the early 14th century, were well known for their wealth and learning across the Islamic world, and even beyond. The trade in gold appears also to have stimulated the growth of forest kingdoms, such as Benin and Oyo. These would grow in importance with the arrival of European ships on the coast in the 15th century. Far to the east, the kingdom of Ethiopia maintained its isolated Christian tradition, again with power based on trade with the north by way of the Nile.

There was also traffic in gold and slaves down the coast of East Africa. The unique stone ruins of Zimbabwe provide evidence to support the reports of inland states in this region.

America.

America was the last continent to be settled by man and it remained the most isolated. Traditional hunter/gatherer lifestyles were successfully followed by people of widely differing culture across wide areas of North America and within the many forest regions of North America until they suffered under the impact of European invaders. The cultivation of maize and then of other crops, however, made possible the development of more complex civilizations.

Central America. The earliest civilization was that of the Olmecs, which flourished on the coast of the Gulf of Mexico in the 7th century BC Many of the characteristics of later civilizations of the region can already be recognized in these people. In their capital of Teotihuacan they built huge pyramids, apparently dedicated to the same gods which would be worshipped by people of the region in later generations.

The most accomplished civilization of the region was the Maya, centred on the Yukatan peninsula, which reached its peak in the 9th century BC The Mayans used a pictogram form of writing. Like the Babylonians, they laid emphasis on the calendar and the heavenly bodies and they developed great skill in mathematics and astronomy, working out the duration of the year and learning how to predict eclipses. They were the first people in the world's history to achieve a sense of the vast span of time. Mayan sites, like those of ancient Egypt, are not cities, but vast complexes of temples and other ceremonial buildings.

The Maya were succeeded by the Toltecs, and they were overthrown in their turn by the Aztecs, who dominated the region from the 13th century. They appear to have been the first to introduce mass human sacrifice. This practice came to dominate the whole of Aztec strategy for the region. As victims were best found in warfare, they had no motivation to create conditions of peace, but rather encouraged a general unrest among subject people.

The Aztecs had a tradition that the white skinned and bearded god Quetzalcoatl would one day return from the east. When the invading Spaniards appeared to fulfil this prophesy, there were many subject people who were prepared to take their side against their feared Aztec masters.

The Andes. The long spine of the Andes is perhaps the most improbable setting for any of the world's civilizations. Between 600 and 1000 AD a people called the Huari brought some political unity to this area. In the 12th century, the Inca, based on Cuzco in modern Peru, were only one of many smaller groupings. They then conquered an empire which by the 15th century stretched 2000 miles from Quito in modern Equador to the deserts of Chile.

The Incas were a non-literate people. Instructions were carried to distant parts of the empire by messengers. Again, lacking the wheel, these messengers travelled on foot over a road network, built with great engineering skill. Inca power was centred on heavily fortified cities, where invading Spaniards were to find a wealth of beautiful objects made of gold and stone.

The Incas were not as oppressive to their subject people as the Aztecs, but there were still many who were prepared to support the small force of Spaniards who arrived in 1531 to conquer and loot the empire.

5. The Triumph of Europe.

The Background to Conquest.

New Perspectives. The Mappa Mundi, in Hereford Cathedral, illustrates the medieval perspective of the world. Jerusalem lies in the centre of the world, with the three known continents – Asia, Africa and Europe – arranged around the Mediterranean Sea. Phoenician and Viking ships may have sailed the wider oceans, but these lay at the edge of the known universe.

By the 15th century, changes were taking place. The reports of Marco Polo's travels in the East were becoming widely known. No profit orientated merchant could ignore his descriptions of markets loaded with silks, velvets and damasks. He had travelled beyond China to the islands of the Pacific and described how cheaply spices could be obtained. It was still impossible to keep meat animals alive through the European winter, so all except the breeding stock was slaughtered and salted down at Michaelmas. By spring it was barely edible without pepper, cinnamon and nutmeg to disguise the taste.

In 1400 also a copy of the Hellenistic Ptolemy's *Geography* was brought from Constantinople and published in the west. It contained many errors, but did show that the world was round and not a flat dish. During the century, this became the accepted view of scholars.

The Ottoman conquests helped stimulate interest in alternative routes to East Asia. Thorough medieval times the majority of luxury goods had been brought by the Asian overland routes. These were now threatened by a hostile power. The Genoese, traditional allies of Byzantium, were particularly threatened by the new developments. Ottomans and Venetians alike combined to shut them out from the profitable business.

Logic demanded that traders should turn their attention to the oceans that lay beyond the enclosed Mediterranean world. Luxury goods were high value and low bulk cargo. Projected returns on investment on one cargo reaching Europe were astronomical.

Technical advance. During the 15th century major technical advances were also made in Europe, which brought such a project within the bounds of the possible. Before that time European ships had been square rigged on a single main mast. Such a ship could be manned by a small crew, but could not sail efficiently into the wind. Arab ships used a lateen sail. This could sail into the wind, but such a large crew was needed that it could never go far from land where food could be obtained. Ship

97

builders now constructed multi-masted vessels, with both square and lateen sails, which could both be handled by a small crew and sail into the wind.

If ships were to sail far out from land, then navigational techniques needed to improve. By 1500 European sailors were skilled in the use of the magnetic compass, either re-invented or brought from China, and in measuring latitude. Almost 200 years more years would pass before similar advances were made in calculating longitude. Great advances were also made in cartographical techniques, with the Dutch leading the way.

European craftsmen also developed gunnery to new levels. King John II of Portugal took particular interest in the problems of mounting modern guns on board ship. Success in these experiments meant that European ships could command the seas. In previous centuries ships came together with grappling hooks to allow soldiers to fight a conventional battle. Now the European ship could sink an enemy ship without allowing it to come close enough to bring the soldiers into action.

Population and Prices. The intellectual climate was favourable, commercial incentives were strong, and the required technology was available. As with Norsemen and Mongols, however, a further 'push factor' was needed to trigger off a major movement of European people. Demographers have shown that Western Europe had recovered from the Black Death and a cyclical population increase was in progress. Pauperism was on the increase, and also, in populations organised on the basis of primogeniture, landless younger sons of gentry families were looking for any way of making a fortune.

Historians now link the population rise with an inflationary trend which persisted through the 16th century. On average, prices quadrupled between 1500 and 1600. Since wages and savings did not always keep up with the rising prices, this created conditions of hardship which could make emigration attractive.

Religion. Christians of the period generally held that unbelievers possessed no rights. The Pope declared that Christian kings had a right to conquer heathen lands. Some Catholic friars and, later, Jesuits did identify with the cause of the native people, but even their mission stations were instruments of colonial control. The Protestant record was, if anything, worse. 300 years would pass before protestant Christians made any serious attempt to protect the rights of and to share their faith with non European people.

Asia.

The Portuguese. By 1400 Portugal was free from Moslem rule and had established itself as a separate country from Spain. Its geographical position made it a natural Atlantic pioneer. In the first half of the 15th century, the king's brother, Henry 'The Navigator' established a school for sailors at Sagres, by Cape St. Vincent, and sent out expeditions to explore ever further south into the Atlantic. Slowly they pushed the boundaries of exploration beyond the Azores and to Senegal.

In 1487, 27 years after Henry's death, Bartholomew Diaz rounded the Cape of Good Hope and established that the way to India lay clear. In 1498 Vasco da Gama took his ship to Calicut in south India. Indian merchants were happy to sell to the newcomers as they offered higher prices than the Arabs. He returned with a cargo of pepper, cinnamon, ginger, cloves and tin. It was reported that the King of Portugal and Vasco da Gama's other backers made a 6000% return on their investment. A century of human and financial investment had finally paid it dividend. In 1503 the Portuguese established a permanent base in India, at Cochin, followed in 1510 by Goa, and later by Seurat.

In 1509 the Arabs sent a fleet, manned by 15,000 men, to drive the Portuguese from their seas, but the European superiority in ships and gunnery proved decisive in a battle off Diu. From that time European fleets exercised control over the world's oceans. Arab and oriental sailors could no longer confront them in battle, but only operate as pirates.

In 1517 the first Portuguese ship arrived off the coast of China and according to European custom fired their guns in salute. The Chinese found these barbaric Europeans 'crafty and cruel', but had to respect their guns which 'shook the earth'. In 1521 Portuguese ships had reached the Spice Islands. In 1557 they established their trading base at Macao, off the Chinese mainland.

The Dutch. The Portuguese successfully protected their Africa route against encroachment by other European nations until the last years of the 16th century. Then in 1594 a group of Dutch businessmen fitted out four ships to sail to the Far East. They carried the products of Europe – woollen and linen fabrics, glassware, ornaments and different kinds of ironware, including armour. The ships reached East Asia and found that the people welcomed their quality goods. In 1602, the Dutch parliament, the Estates, set up the Dutch East India Company to follow up this initiative. The Malacca Strait, in modern Indonesia, became the focus of the empire, with headquarters on the island of Java. The Dutch then set about driving the Portuguese out of their Asian empire. Only a few Portuguese outposts, such a Goa and Macao survived the assault.

Once in control, the Dutch traders ruthlessly set about eliminating all competition. In 1623 ten English merchants were tortured and killed at Amboyna. But they were not content to exclude other European competition from their market. Chinese junks were shut out of their traditional markets as even local trade was channelled into Dutch ships. By now Europe was becoming glutted with spices, so the Dutch governor, Jan Coen set about controlling production to keep prices high. On one occasion he destroyed all the nutmeg trees on the Banda Islands and either killed or sold into slavery the entire population of 15,000 people. He burnt villages along the coast of China in an attempt to control the whole region, but complained that China, like India, was 'too extensive for discipline'.

The English. The English East India Company was founded two years earlier than the Dutch, but it lost the race to control the Spice Islands. After Amboyna, the Dutch and the English were bitter commercial rivals. The English had to accept that the prize of the Pacific trade was closed to them and had to make do as a second best with establishing themselves in India. The trade in coffee, tea and cotton goods was of lower value than that from further east, but the English trading stations at Madras, Bombay and Calcutta grew in importance tea gained status as a fashionable drink. When Dutch power waned in the later years of the 17th century, English ships were able to use their Indian bases for trading with China and the Pacific Islands.

The French. The French East India Company had now replaced the Dutch as the main competition. French merchants, however, operated under difficulties. They came from a nation whose power was centred on its land army. While naval and commercial interests were influential in London, they carried little weight in Paris. In time of war, French ships were exposed to the powerful English navy and French overseas outposts were at all times starved of resources.

It long seemed impossible that any European nation would establish political control in the sub continent. Then the death of Aurangzeb in 1707 marked the end of the Mogul Empire as an effective force, and the sub-continent split into warring states. From that time, the trading companies became increasingly became in politics.

America.

The Spanish. On January 2nd 1492 the troops of the 'Catholic Monarchs' Isabella of Castile and her husband, Ferdinand of Aragon finally drove the Moors out of Grenada. In the cheering crowd was a Genoese sailor, Christopher Columbus. Like another Genoese, John Cabot, he had decided that the Indes could best be reached by sailing westwards. Both turned to western European monarchs, with a natural interest in Atlantic trade. Columbus won the support of Isabella and in August his three ships sailed from Palos, to reach San Salvador on 12 October.

Columbus was bitterly disappointed that he did not find the eastern markets described by Marco Polo. In later voyages he explored the Caribbean Islands and reached the mainland. He died in 1506, still convinced that he had reached the Indes. Before then, however, another Italian, Amerigo Vespucci, this time in Portuguese pay, had established that this was indeed the continent which subsequently carried his name. In the year that Columbus sailed, the Spanish Pope, Alexander VI issued a Bull, awarding to Spain and Portugal all lands already discovered or to be discovered 'in the West, towards the Indes or the ocean seas, with the dividing line between the two on the line of longitude 45° West. This ruling gave Brazil to Portugal and the rest of the continent to Spain. The Spanish, however, never established effective control to the north of a line from modern Georgia in the east to California in the west.

In 1519 Magellan led an expedition to explore this new world. When the remains of his expedition returned in 1522, having circumnavigated the globe, the basic facts of world geography were finally established.

Meanwhile the Spaniards were establishing their power in the New World. In 1513 Balboa crossed the Isthmus of Panama and reached the Pacific Ocean. In the east, Portuguese guns could win naval battles, but they could never bring down great empires. In the west, however, the Spaniards found that civilizations crumbled before them. There was too large a gap between the technology of the 'New World' on one side and the firearms, horses and armour of the 'Old World' on the other. Perhaps most important, the American 'Indian' people were psychologically ill equipped to confront the brutal European soldiers. Many were killed by the newcomers; many lost the will to live when forced to work in unfamiliar ways; even more died of the plague and other diseased for which they lacked immunity. According to one estimate, 25 million people lived in what was to become New Spain when Columbus landed, but only $1^1/2$ million survived a century later.

The Spaniards may not have found silks and spices, but they found gold. What to the native Americans was a decorative metal was, to the Spaniards, the basic unit of exchange and measurement of wealth. For gold Cortes and Pizarro destroyed the Aztec and Inca civilizations. Unsuccessful searches for gold established Spanish rule in what is now the south of the United States, from Florida to the Great Plains, and the Californian coast. All kinds of gold objects were melted down and shipped back to Spain, where the new riches funded the emergence of Spain as a major power.

The gold was soon plundered and no significant mines were discovered. A sustainable flow of wealth was, however, established by the opening of silver mines in Peru. Spain now controlled both sides of the Isthmus of Panama and a merchant fleet was built on the westward, Pacific side. A trading base was established at Manila in the Philippines, and galleons carried trading goods across the wide Pacific. These luxury goods from the Orient, along with silver from Peru, were then carried across the Isthmus of Panama and loaded onto the Atlantic treasure fleet for Spain.

In the early years of colonization few women left Spain for the New World, and settlers took Indian wives. The culture, and even the religion of New Spain therefore developed a syncretism between Spanish and Indian traditions. In time the importation of black slaves from Africa further complicated the ethnic mix. It has, however, remained generally true into modern times that the social position and wealth of any individual could be gauged by skin colour.

The English. John Cabot was convinced that Columbus had got his sums wrong. He believed correctly that China was far out of range of any ship following a southerly route. By his calculation, the journey could be made at a more northerly latitude. Sailors from Bristol, England were already fishing the Newfoundland banks and knew the North Atlantic well. Cabot therefore won support from King Henry VII of England and in 1496 reached the coast of North America. It was not obvious that the north of the continent was embedded in the Arctic ice and Cabot's son, Sebastian led a long line of English sailors in search of the North West Passage. The English sea dogs, Drake and Hawkins preferred the warm waters of New Spain to the cold northern seas.

They first operated as traders, and then, after being attacked by Spaniards, as privateers.

The gold of New Spain and the luxury trade of the Orient offered instant riches. Returns on investment in North America were likely to be less spectacular. By the 1580s, however Sir Walter Raleigh and others were advocating colonization of the land of Virginia, which was now claimed by England. Attempts were made to establish colonies in 1585 and 1589, but both failed. The first successful colony was established at Jamestown in 1607. In 1620 a group of 'Pilgrim' refugees set up a colony at New Plymouth, Massachusetts, and later moved to the better site of Boston.

The English settlements were based on a farming economy. Disease, spreading from New Spain had recently ravaged the native American tribes, leaving much of the land vacant. The surviving people practised a mixed hunting and farming economy, based on shifting cultivation, so to newcomers much of the land appeared to be empty. As land hungry settlers kept on arriving and pushing inland towards the Appalachian Mountains conflict with the Indian people was inevitable.

The Dutch. In 1614 the United New Netherlands Company established a colony at the mouth of the Hudson River. The Dutch recognized the potential of the trade in beaver fur and used the Hudson to make contact with Indian people of the interior. This settlement divided the English colonies of Virginia and New England and hostility between the two Protestant countries, aroused in the far Spice Islands, spilled over in the New World. In 1664 the English drove the Dutch from North America.

At the height of their powers, the Dutch carried their assault on the Portuguese Empire into the New World by annexing Brazil in 1637. The Portuguese settlers rebelled against them and they were driven out in 1654, leaving Brazil as the western outpost of a once great Portuguese Empire.

The French. In 1603 the French explorer de Champlain sailed into the St. Lawrence River. He too was still searching for the elusive route to the east. He established settlements which were to become Montreal and Quebec and pressed on to explore the inland waterways of the interior. The French settlers were comparatively few in number and they received little support from their home government. Champlain and those who came after him exploited Indian rivalries to establish a flourishing trading empire, based on the fashion trade in beaver fur. As the animals were hunted to near extinction in the east, the 'beaver frontier' moved west, taking the hardy French after them.

French explorers followed the Great Lakes waterway into the interior and then the Mississippi to the Gulf of Mexico. Here they established the French outpost of New Orleans. The North American empire, named Louisiana, after Louis XIV, now followed the waterways in a huge, but lightly populated arc. At first the French and English colonists only came into contact with each other in the Hudson Valley. The risk of conflict grew, however, when the French tightened the noose around the English colonies by taking control of the Ohio River. At the time, however, colonial wars, which decided the fate of India and North America, were seen as little more than a sideshow beside the main European conflicts.

The Old Colonial System. The Dutch can be credited with the development of mercantilism, which became known as the old colonial system. This was not developed specifically for North America, but, when applied by the English in their American possessions, it became a root cause of later conflict between the colonists and the mother country. It was assumed that overseas colonies existed to promote the interests of the mother country, by extending its economic base. Colonists were expected to produce cash crops. Some, like rice from the Carolinas or tobacco from Virginia, could not be produced in northern Europe. Softwood timber from New England was also of vital strategic importance for ship building at a time when European forests were finally disappearing. Buying these goods from a national source saved the mother country the foreign exchange, which would be required to purchase them from abroad. By selling these crops, the colonists earned money, which would be spent on the

manufactured goods. This in turn assisted the manufac-
turing industries and strengthened the merchant marine
of the mother country. Any business between the colony
and a third country had to transacted through the mother
country. This had the further benefit of boosting customs
revenue.

The trade-off was that the mother country was responsible for providing the colonists with protection, be
it from local populations or from hostile Europeans. This
involved the Westminster government in the expense of
funding wars against the French and their Indian allies.
The system came under pressure when the colonies
began to develop out of their original role as providers of
raw materials to develop their own manufactures.

Africa.

The Atlantic Slave Trade. The Portuguese were the
first to discover that West Africa had human resources,
which were to be exploited in a slave trade, which
continued for some 350 years. A base was established on
the coast as early as 1448, from which comparatively
small numbers of slaves were shipped back to Portugal.

An acute labour problem then began to develop in
the new American plantations. The obvious solution was
to recruit American Indians. Heavy field work, however,
proved alien to them. Many died, often by suicide, when
forced to work on European plantations. European la-

bour was also brought in, both by the forcible transportation of convicts, and by indentured labour schemes, under which immigrants were bound to their masters for a given number of years. Again, however, expectation of life was short, and the labour problem remained unresolved.

Portuguese ships then began to take slaves direct to their colony of Brazil. In 1562 John Hawkins began the English slave trade between West Africa and the Caribbean. Dutch, French, Danes and later sailors from both North and South America joined in the business. European nations established forts on the West African coast to protect the interests of their slave traders.

It is estimated that some eight to ten million slaves were carried across the Middle Passage to America. The economies of European cities, such as Nantes, Bristol and later Liverpool were based on slaving, and the business was accepted as a part of the national commercial interest.

The individual suffering of slaves would ultimately receive wide publicity; the impact the trade had on African society is harder to quantify. European sailors rarely penetrated inland to find their own captives. Domestic slavery already existed on the continent, and Africans initially sold their own slaves to purchase European goods. In time, however, demand outstripped this source of supply. Military confederacies, such as

111

Dahomey and Ashanti, grew up to fulfil the double function of protecting their own members, and feeding slaves to the European forts. When Europeans later penetrated the continent, they discovered that these states often acted with a savagery untypical of African society further inland. The demand for slaves created an endemic state of war which penetrated inland, far beyond any direct European contact. The resulting depopulation appears, however, to have been largely balanced by improvements in the African diet as a result of the importation of American crops, such as the yam and cassava.

Colonization. The first African colonies had the prime function of protecting and providing staging posts for national ships on the eastern trade routes. The Portuguese early established the outposts in Mozambique and Angola which would achieve the distinction of being the longest lasting European overseas colonies. In 1652 Jan van Riesbeck set up the Dutch colony at the Cape of Good Hope, to serve the eastern convoys as a 'tavern of the seas'. In the 18th century, the French established an interest in the Indian Ocean island of Madagascar, along with Mauritius, and Reunion. The slave coast of West Africa remained unattractive for colonization. European slavers and soldiers themselves suffered a high mortality rate from tropical diseases, particularly yellow fever and malaria.

East Africa. At this time, East Africa lay off the main trading routes, and the region offered little to attract European merchants. Arab dhows still sailed undisturbed to Zanzibar and their caravans penetrated deep inland. Here again, slaves featured prominently as a trading commodity alongside gold and ivory. The area remained an Arab area of influence until European missionaries and traders penetrated the area in the 19th century.

6. The Nations of Europe

Italy and the European Powers.

The City States and the Papacy. In the 15th century, the northern half of Italy was the most advanced part of Europe. The great trading cities of Genoa and Venice brought in wealth and broad contact was maintained, both through trade and cultural exchange with Arab and Byzantine civilizations. The country probably benefited from the fact that it was never brought under unitary political control.

The broken terrain of Tuscany and Umbria suited the development of independent city states, not unlike those of ancient Greece. Florence and Sienna, like Athens and Sparta of old, built up confederacies to counterbalance the power of the other. In the late 14th century, the banking family of Medici took power in Florence. Times were not always easy, but they led the city to its unique flowering of culture.

In the north another ring of states, with Milan as the most powerful, controlled the trading routes across the Alps. In the centre, the pope ruled the Papal States as any other temporal monarch, and involved himself in the politics of the peninsula, attempting always to extend the patrimony of St. Peter. During this period the lifestyle of the popes was little different from that of any other monarch. They led troops into battle, promoted family interests, including those of their children, and built themselves enormous monuments. Julius II's decision to build himself a tomb set off the chain of events which triggered the Reformation in distant Germany; the tomb would be too large for St. Peter's, so the church had to be rebuilt; this involved raising money by the granting of indulgences.

The Theory of Kingship. Within this turbulent world of Italian politics, only the fittest survived. Nicolo Machiavelli worked for the Florentine state, travelling widely as a diplomat. He wrote a book, called *The Prince*, which was based on these experiences, which contained advice for the Medici family on the theory and practice of government. Political decisions, he argued, could only be taken on a cool, indeed callous, assessment of the security needs of the state and of its ruler. Medieval concepts of the mutual duties of ruler and subjects were cut away in this first exposition of what would later come to be called 'real politik'.

Medieval monarchy was based on a feudal alliance between king and his tenants in chief. In the 16th century power was being drawn to the centre, at the expense of both the magnates and of representational institutions. For Machiavelli's prince, power was its own justification. The theory of centralization was later taken further with the formulation of the concept of the divine right of kings. Rulers, it was said, held power directly from God. Rebellion was a sin and criticism of the royal will was tantamount to treason.

Foreign Invasion. In 1494 Charles VIII of France crossed the Alps at the head of an army of 30,000 men. He laid claim to the Kingdom of Naples and on his way south, through Rome itself, his army left a trail of destruction. Other foreign armies followed. Artists still worked on, producing some of the greatest works known to man, but the days of the city state were over and Italy would henceforth be a pawn in the real politik of the great powers. In 1527 the ragged, unpaid and hungry army of the great emperor, Charles V, ran wild in the streets of Rome, and the city was sacked for the first time since the barbarian invasions.

The Empire of Charles V. Throughout medieval times, kingship was fundamentally a matter of family inheritance. Charles was the ultimate beneficiary of this dynastic system. From his mother, the mad Joanna, he inherited his grandparents' crowns of Castile and Aragon. On the paternal side, he inherited from his grandfather the title of Holy Roman Emperor, and from his grandmother the lands of the Duchy of Burgundy. As king of

Castile he controlled Spanish land in the New World; as Emperor he ruled Austria, Hungary, Bohemia and much of Germany; as Duke of Burgundy he possessed the Netherlands, which was the richest part of all Europe. His empire was larger than that of Charlemagne.

France was now shut in on all sides, and its king was determined not to let Italy fall to Charles' empire. The crusading spirit was finally laid to rest as Pope and King of France allied with the Ottoman Turks against Charles.

This great empire, like that of Charlemagne, carried the seeds of its own destruction. Charles was unable to function adequately as ruler of such dispersed lands, and resentment grew, particularly in the Netherlands at the taxes raised to support Italian wars. Charles was also depressed at his inability to control the spread of protestantism within his own lands. He abdicated in 1556 and the empire was divided. The title of Emperor passed to his brother Ferdinand I, while the more valuable western share, consisting of Spain and the old Burgundian lands, went to his son, Philip II. There were now two Hapsburg dynasties in Europe.

Protestantism and the Counter Reformation.

The Spread of Protestantism. Luther's new beliefs found most followers in northern Europe, particularly in Germany itself and in Scandinavia. The impetus behind the further spread of protestantism came, not from Germany, but from Geneva. John Calvin was French, but he achieved prominence in the Swiss canton. He preached a harsh form of protestantism; since God was all powerful, he had predestined a minority of people – the elect – to salvation and the rest to damnation. The elect had to show their status by a strict adherence to a way of life. Within Geneva moral sins, like adultery and even disobedience by a child to parents were severely punished. Calvinism proved to be a more militant faith than Lutheranism. It appealed in the Netherlands, in England and on the west coast of France, in Scotland and later in the Lutheran heartland of Germany.

All Protestantism stressed the direct communion of the individual with God, and it is not therefore surprising that it early showed a capacity to fragment. In 1532 an extreme group, the Anabaptists, took control of the German city of Münster, preaching not only rejection of infant baptism, but polygamy and a radical social gospel. In the extreme Protestant sects, authority lay not in any higher political or ecclesiastical power, but in the local 'gathered church'. These separatist churches were persecuted in Protestant and Catholic countries alike, but it was this tradition that would ultimately implant itself in the New England colonies of North America, and profoundly influence the development of American society.

Toleration was not a cherished ideal in 16th century Europe, but by 1530 it had become clear that protestantism was too powerful a movement to be readily suppressed. In that year the Peace of Augsburg laid down the principle of 'cuius regio, eius religio' – the country would follow the religion of the ruler. This left rulers free to persecute within their own dominions.

Sweden and England Break with Rome. Two European monarchs took their nations out of communion with the Roman church. Both were motivated by national and financial, rather than by religious reasons. In 1523 the young Swedish nobleman, Gustavus Vasa, succeeded in his struggle to make Sweden independent from Denmark, and was proclaimed king. Lutheranism had already made progress among his people. In 1527 he broke with Rome as a symbol of the new national independence, and he enriched his hard pressed government with church lands.

Henry VIII of England had showed no personal inclination towards the reformed religion; indeed he had written a pamphlet attacking Luther, and had persecuted Protestants. In 1530, however, he became involved in a dispute with the pope over his divorce to Catherine of Aragon. Using selective intimidation, he won the support of parliament for a breach with Rome, and then for the plundering of the monastic lands. The Church of England, reformed in doctrine, but conservative in practice, was the creation of Henry's Archbishop of Canterbury, Thomas Cranmer. After a short return to catholicism under Mary I, Henry's daughter, Elizabeth, declared that the English church should be a home for all men of goodwill. Separatist Protestants and politically active Catholics were still persecuted, but England did escape the worst violence of these years.

The Counter Reformation. The Roman church had been on the defensive against an aggressive protestantism for 25 years when Pope Paul III called his bishops together for the Council of Trent. Paul represented a new generation of Pope, anxious to clear away the scandals of the past, and re-establish the western church on a firm footing. The discussions were dominated by bishops from Spain and Italy, where protestantism had found no foothold. The Council brought in reforms – indulgences, for instance, were abolished – but it made no concessions to Protestant faith. By the time that the Council had finished its debates in 1563, the lines of division were clearly drawn.

Catholicism was now on the counter offensive. As in the past, monasticism provided the papacy with its front line troops. In 1540, Ignatius Loyola, who had been a fellow student in Paris with John Calvin, established the Society of Jesus, or Jesuits. Members were bound to total loyalty to the Pope, and this provided the reforming papacy with a means of circumventing special interests within the church. Jesuits became particularly prominent in education and in missionary work.

Spain and the Netherlands.

The Expulsions. Even without Charles' eastern lands, Philip II's Spain remained the dominant power in Europe. He controlled southern Italy and Sicily and succeeded in conquering Portugal. Spain's European power was now underpinned by the revenues of a two huge overseas empires.

The nation's weakness was not clearly evident at the time. When the Moors were finally defeated, Moslems and Jews had been promised security within the Christian state. The presence of infidels, however, proved too much for Catholic rulers, still driven by the intolerance of the Inquisition. Moors, Jews, and converted Moors, the Moriscos, were all driven out of the country. These, however, were the very trades people and skilled craftsmen on whom the economy of the nation rested. As a result, Spain became heavily dependent on imported goods, particularly from the prosperous northern Netherlands. On occasions the Panama fleet had to be diverted and sailed direct to unload its treasure in the Netherlands.

The Spanish Netherlands. The old Burgundian lands covered both of the modern states of Belgium and Holland. The greatest centres of prosperity, with Antwerp outstanding, lay in the south. The northern part, mostly consisting of land drained from the Rhine delta, contained the finest farmland in Europe, but, even with intensive agriculture, it could not feed the growing towns. Calvinist protestantism had won adherents both in the north and in the south.

Charles V was born in the Netherlands and during his reign the two religions co-existed with reasonable tolerance. The accession of Spanish born Philip II, however, brought change. As king, he was determined to bring the old Burgundian noble families under his control, and, as a faithful son of the church, he meant to stamp out heresy in his land. The Spanish Duke of Alva was sent with an army to bring the area under control.

Dutch Independence. In 1572 William Prince of Orange led the People of the Netherlands in revolt. As Spanish armies established control of the south, many Protestants moved north behind the protection of the dykes, and the religious division between the Catholic south and the Protestant north was established. In 1581 the followers of William of Orange declared their independence from Spain. No matter how bitter the fighting, the trade between Spain and her rebellious provinces never ceased. Philip was in no position to cut off this channel of supplies for his people and the Dutch were happy to drain the enemy of wealth. William was murdered on Philip's orders in 1584, but the struggle continued until Spain made a truce in 1609. Almost forty years would pass before Spain finally recognized the independence of the Dutch people, but in practice Holland had established its independence from its traditional ruling house.

The Dutch Republic. The new nation was unique in that power was based on trade, rather than on inherited land. A successful Dutchman did not plan for the day when he would put aside the cares of trade and live as a gentleman; his objective was to hand a thriving business to his heirs. The people lived by a strict work ethic, and made the most of the limited resources of their small land.

National wealth was founded on north – south trade, carrying products such as grain, timber and iron from the Baltic to the overpopulated Mediterranean lands. Dutch flyboats, little more than floating holds, plied the oceans. 'Norway was their forest, the banks of the Rhine and the Dordogne their vineyard; Spain and Ireland grazed their sheep; India and Arabia were their gardens and the sea their highway.' Scholars also provided vital information for the sailors and, in doing so, laid the foundation of modern geography.

The Decline of Spain. The loss of the Netherlands was the clearest marker of Spain's fall from the position of Europe's dominant power. In 1588 a Spanish naval Armada was also defeated by the English fleet. In 1640 Portugal re-established her independence under the house of Breganza. The nation could have overcome military reverse; the basic problem was that Philip II and his successors concentrated on military and colonial affairs at the expense of the economy which had been shattered by the mass expulsions.

The French Wars of Religion.

The French Monarchy. In the middle of the 16th century, French royal power stood at a low ebb. Financial stringency led to offices being sold to the highest bidder, and, partly as a result, the size and independence of the aristocracy was ever increasing. Calvinism was strong in Brittany and Normandy, and growing in power further south on the Atlantic coast, and in Languedoc Its strength was based on craftsmen and some poorer nobles, followed by a growing number of peasants. By 1562 there were over 1500 'Huguenot' congregations, many led by Geneva trained pastors. The Catholics themselves were divided into two parties – the moderates, led by the Regent, Catherine de Medici, who planned to keep the peace by giving a measure of toleration to the Protestants, and an extreme Catholic party, who wanted to see heresy stamped out.

The Wars. Fighting broke out after extremist Catholics massacred Huguenot congregation at Vassy in 1562. The ensuing wars were fought with great ferocity on both sides. In 1572 3,000 Huguenots were massacred in Paris on St. Bartholomew's Day and in 1588 the king was ejected from his own capital by extreme Catholics. In

1584 the Huguenot Henry of Navarre became heir to the throne. He succeeded in bringing the war to an end by turning Catholic and reaching agreement with his former Protestant followers in the Edict of Nantes. This left the Huguenots with freedom of worship in large areas of the country, as well as certain fortified cities. These now effectively lay outside the royal control.

Germany.

The Empire after Charles V. Charles V's brother Ferdinand saw himself as a faithful Catholic and soldier of the Counter Reformation. His own lands, and the south of Germany remained Catholic. The Protestant forces set against him were divided. In the north were the Lutheran powers of Denmark, Saxony and Brandenburg. The Calvinist stronghold lay to the west around the Rhine. Ferdinand dreamed of winning back the whole of Germany to catholicism, while at the same time bringing it once again under imperial rule.

Ferdinand was unable to achieve his ambition because his empire was exposed on its eastern flank. In the south, the Ottoman Empire reached the peak of its power under Suleiman 1, and even threatened Vienna itself. In the north, Sweden was establishing control of the Baltic Sea while Poland and Russia both pressed on German land.

The Thirty Years War. In the early 17th century the

religious divisions became more sharply fixed. In 1608-9 the Catholic League and the Calvinist Union were set up as rival military blocks. The first of a series of wars broke out in 1618, when the Calvinist Elector Palatine was elected King of Bohemia. The Catholic armies, led by virtually independent war lords, won early successes, but this rallied the Lutheran armies to the Protestant cause. The Protestant champion turned out to be Gustavus Adolphus, King of Sweden, who won a series of battles before he was killed at Lützen in 1632.

By this time the religious battle lines were becoming blurred. Catholic France, under Cardinal Richelieu, was prepared to fund Protestant armies and even to intervene directly to prolong the war and so prevent and re-emergence of imperial power in Germany. This brought in Catholic and Hapsburg Spain on the imperial side.

The war was a disaster for the people of Germany. Roaming armies stripped the countryside of food; the devastation caused by the imperial sack of Magdeburg in 1629 rivalled that of a Mongol army. When the war limped to a close in 1648 the countryside was impoverished and depopulated. Ferdinand's ideal of a Catholic Germany, united under the empire was destroyed. Protestantism was unassailable in the north and the effective power of the emperor in the German speaking lands was henceforth limited to his Austrian heartland. In the Treaties of Westphalia the Emperor had to accept the independence of Switzerland – a reality since the end of the 15th century – and the King of Spain that of the Netherlands. France and Spain both made achieved territorial gains in German lands. Most significant for the future, the new power of Brandenburg had emerged in the north.

Brandenburg – Prussia. In 1640 'The Great Elector' Frederick William, of the House of Hohenzollern, inherited Brandenburg and the eastern territory of Prussia. A man of great energy, he set about creating a well run, modern state. His twin tools were an efficient civil service and a highly disciplined army, which served as a model for later German armies. The Great Elector's work was consolidated a century later by Frederick II 'the Great'. He had no vision of a united Germany, but he ruthlessly expanded his family lands at the expense of the Empire.

The Hegemony of France.

Richelieu. Henry IV was assassinated in 1610, leaving a country at peace, but with many problems. The Huguenots were a state within a state; the nobles were over powerful and contributed little to the national life; the peasants were desperately poor and over taxed.

In 1624 his successor, Louis XIII, appointed Cardinal Richelieu as head of the royal council. For 18 years, he worked single mindedly to establish royal power within the nation. He had no wish to persecute the Protestants, but he destroyed the independent Huguenot fortresses. He made examples at high level to bring the nobles under his control. Regional government was delegated to directly appointed intendants, who exercised the complete range of royal power.

Richlieu's foreign policy was directed at limiting the power of Spain and improving national security by achieving 'natural frontiers' at the Rhine and the Alps. For this, he was prepared to ally with Protestants and to prolong the misery of the Thirty Years War.

Richelieu represented the apotheosis of the Machiavellian ideal; his policy was driven by a cold analysis of *raison d' etat*. He did not, however, recognize that some improvement in the lot of the poor was essential if the state was to be securely based. Shortly after Richelieu and his royal master died in 1642-3, there was a series of popular uprisings across the country, which were known as the Frondes.

Louis XIV. The young king who succeeded was to rule the country until 1715. His domestic and foreign policy was a continuation of that laid down by Richelieu. All real power lay in the hands of non-noble ministers and the intendants, while the nobles were emasculated by being drawn into the glittering court of Versailles.

Unlike Richelieu, however, Louis determined that he would not rule over heretics. He revoked the Edict of

Nantes, facing protestants with the choice of conversion or expulsion. Like Isabella of Castille, he was hereby driving a productive group out of the nation. Economic conditions did improve, but the poor continued to suffer harshly enforced penal taxation.

Much tax revenue was spent on foreign wars. As France had organized leagues to limit the power of Spain, so now others united to contain France. The driving force in the anti-French Grand Alliance was William of Orange, Stadholder of the Netherlands. His power strengthened when, in 1688 he also became king of England as William III. The War of the Grand Alliance (1689-97) was followed by the War of the Spanish Succession (1701-14), which sought to prevent Louis from unifying the crowns of Fence and Spain by dynastic succession.

18th Century France. In 1715 France was clearly the leading power in Europe. Major losses of overseas territory to England in India and North America during the Seven Years War (1756-73) did not appear as significant at the time as they were later to become. Financial weakness, however, underlay the pageantry of the France monarchy. The huge noble class – estimated at up to 250,000 strong – had lost political power, but not financial and legal privilege. The state sank ever more deeply in debt, but had no means of tapping the huge reserves of noble wealth. Here lay the seeds of revolution.

England.

Sea Power. When Roman soldiers were posted to Britain, they considered that they were being consigned to the edge of the civilized world. Through medieval times, the British Isles remained on the periphery of the known world. The discovery of America moved the centre of gravity away from the Mediterranean, towards the Atlantic Ocean. Geography therefore now favoured England.

As an island nation, the English were perforce a seafaring people. By 1500, however, this seafaring tradition had not, however, been converted into naval power. The defeat of the Spanish Armada in 1588 proved to be a turning point. The battle was won by strategy, rather than by fighting force, but the Elizabethan sea-dogs created a national myth, which would survive into modern times. Governments, reluctant to involve troops in European land battles, laid the greatest stress on building up naval power and securing naval supplies. The navy provided protection for the island, maintained links with overseas colonies, and secured trade routes against competition.

Monarchy and Parliament. The Tudor monarchs, Henry VIII and his daughter Elizabeth dominated 16th century English politics. The English nobility were few in number, and were generally content to concentrate their efforts on field sports and the efficient management of their estates. While parliamentary government was withering on the continent, in England the old institutions remained robust. Henry found it convenient to use the House of Commons as his ally against the Church, and Elizabeth was able to manage parliament, even if sometimes with difficulty, both as a source of revenue, and as a channel of government.

When Elizabeth died in 1603, the succession passed to the Scots House of Stuart, which, through family and cultural ties, was more influenced by the French model. Very early, James I became involved in disputes with both the legal and parliamentary establishment. James proclaimed the divine right of kings, which, he claimed, gave the king the power to appoint and dismiss judges and to raise taxes. Jurists recovered documents such as Magna Carta from obscurity to defend ancient privileges against the new royal pretensions. Implicit in their arguments lay the notion that royal power was derived from the consent of the people – however the people might be defined. The conflict was made more acute by the fact that personality did not match pretention. The Tudors had maintained authority through the force of their personalities, rather than through modern concepts of kingship. James was intelligent but personally unimpressive; his son Charles I was an inadequate recluse.

The Civil War. Charles I soon found himself in direct confrontation with parliament. In 1628 parliament presented a Petition of Right against the use of arbitrary royal power; in 1629 Charles dissolved parliament and began 11 years of direct rule. Many aspects of royal government were unpopular to influential subjects. An attempt was made to impose 'high church' worship, not only on England but also on Calvinist Scotland. An increasing number of cases were heard in royal prerogative courts, rather than in the courts of common law. Direct taxes, such as ship money, were levied without parliamentary approval. It seemed to many as though Charles would soon follow Richelieu's example and centralize all government.

The outbreak of war in Scotland brought financial disaster and Charles was forced to recall parliament in 1640. A struggle for power led to the outbreak of war in 1642. Historians have long argued the economic, religious and social issues which lay behind the conflict; certainly it was very different in nature from the violent upheavals which would later shake France and Russia. Parliamentary power was based in the rich south east, while the king's was centred in the poorer north and west. The parliamentary victory was due both to this difference in resources, and to the leadership of Oliver Cromwell, who emerged as the outstanding general in the conflict. He kept his New Model Army under such firm control that it could march across countryside and leave fields and property as they had been before the army passed.

The Commonwealth. The parliamentary broke into factions after the defeat of the king. In 1648 one faction seized power, with army support and staged the trial of Charles I. The execution of the king in 1649 provoked a shocked response across Europe. No action could have expressed the rejection of divine kingship more vividly. In 1653, Cromwell staged a military coup and assumed power as Lord Protector. Cromwell died in 1658, and a brief attempt was made to continue the protectorate under his son. This failed, however, and in 1660 the army again was responsible for bringing Charles II back to London.

The Glorious Revolution. The saga of the conflict between the Stuarts and their parliaments was not, however, over. Charles was mistrusted, both for his French sympathies and for his leaning towards catholicism, but he still depended on parliament for revenue. In 1685 he was succeeded by his Catholic brother, James II. Three years later James was forced to leave the country, to be replaced by his Protestant daughter, Mary and her husband, the Dutch William of Orange, who exercised the practical power. William was more interested in securing the English alliance against France, than he was in pursuing power struggles with the English parliament. He therefore accepted laws which established that the king would henceforth require parliamentary consent to raise money and keep a standing army in peace time. It was also agreed that he could not alter or suspend any act of parliament.

In 1714 the English throne passed to the German house of Hanover. Since the new king could not speak English, day to day government passed to a prime minister and a cabinet, drawn from the majority party in the House of Commons. Political power had now finally passed from the monarchy to the property owning classes, who were represented in parliament. In the century which followed parliament largely used its power to improve the position of the landowning class, often at the expense of the poor. English politics had, however, run against the European tide, which favoured greater centralization in the hands of the monarch.

The Act of Union. Throughout history, there had been strife between England and her smaller, poorer northern neighbour, Scotland. The union of the crowns in 1603 did not put an end to this. In 1707, however, the two countries became formally united in the Act of Union. Two clan uprisings followed in 1715 and 1745, in favour of the exiled Stuarts, but these were suppressed. Scots engineers, doctors and scholars were shortly after to make a major contribution to the great surge in national prosperity of the united Great Britain.

Russia.

Boyars and Serfs. Across the continent the Russian

state was following a very different pattern of development. The noble boyars held their land from the Tsar in return for defined services. Since Russia had no law of primogeniture, this class was getting ever larger, and most of its members poorer, as estates were split one generation after another. The mass of the people remained in the medieval condition of serfdom. Families were owned by their masters, had no right to move of their own free will and had no redress except in their masters' court.

The relationship of Tsar and boyars was often marked by bloody conflict. Ivan IV 'The Terrible' allied himself with the merchant class and the common people in an attempt to break noble power. He achieved many real reforms before mental disorder led him, in the latter years of his reign, to behaviour which anticipated that of Joseph Stalin in the 20th century.

National Objectives. Russian development was hindered by the lack of a warm weather outlet to the ocean. The port of Archangel was ice bound in winter, and all year the journey round northern Scandinavia was long and dangerous. The port of Rostov in the south was of little use, as long as the Ottomans controlled the mouth of the Sea of Azov, and the Dardanelles. National policy therefore became directed at winning a port on the Baltic Sea. This brought Russia into conflict with the advanced military state of Sweden, which guarded the Baltic as a Swedish lake.

The Russian Tsar could mobilize huge armies, by raising levies, but there was no adequate support structure. Forces were sent to war with the vague hope that they would be able to live off the land. Often countless thousands starved, and those who survived were in no condition to fight the world's most efficient army.

Peter the Great. Peter succeeded to the throne in 1682 at the age of 10, and suffered huge indignities from guards and boyars while still a child. Once a man, he announced his intention to bring his nation up to date and orientate it towards the West. A man of little education, but enormous energy, he imerged himself in every detail of western science and technology. In a famous visit to the west he was equally at home working in disguise as a dock worker in Holland and meeting with scientists in England. His methods of enforcement were effective, if sometimes eccentric.

The vindication of Peter's work came in 1709 when his army won a decisive victory over the Swedish army under Charles XII at Poltava. Russia had won its outlet to the Baltic Sea, and here Peter decided to build his capital of St. Petersburg.

Peter's great failure was that, like Louis XIV in France, he failed to do anything to improve the lot of the Russian poor. Someone had to pay for wars against Turkey and Sweden, for the modern weapons, for new ships and for the fine capital city. The poor were taxed and taxed again until they were left with the barest minimum necessary to keep themselves and their families alive. It is a measure of the depth of the misery and the capacity of the Russian people to absorb suffering that revolution did not erupt in violence for another 200 years.

7. The Western Mind

The Renaissance.

Italy. The word *renaissance* was coined in the 19th century to describe the rebirth in Italy of the classical ideal in art, architecture and letters. The 'Middle Ages' was looked upon as a dark period before the great transformation of the 15th and early 16th centuries. Recent study has shown that the picture was more complicated; classicism remained strong throughout the Middle Ages, and there was more cross fertilization between Europe north and south of the Alps than had been assumed.

Any gallery visitor can, however, see the astonishing change which happened in visual perception within a comparatively few years. Across northern Italy artists experimented with new forms. In the words of Vasari, Giotto 'restored the art of design'. In Umbria, Piero della Francesca used mathematics to work out laws of perspective, well beyond any classical achievement. In Florence, Michelangelo combined an analytical eye with his huge talent to create a new vision of the human – or at least male – form. Even when painters and sculptors continued to work on church commissions, they now used live models to give a new sense of naturalism.

There was a keen awareness among the artistic community that they were living in an exciting new age. The Medici and other patrons commissioned works with secular themes, often drawn from Greek mythology. Artists were no longer faceless craftsmen who had produced so many medieval treasures. Art had found a new self consciousness.

The same, secular driven, innovation was reflected in music and literature. There was a passionate interest in all aspects of antiquity. Some sculptors even buried their own work and dug it up again, claiming it as a classical discovery. Old manuscripts were found in monastic libraries or brought from the east and studied with a new intensity. Enthusiasm for antiquity did not preclude Christian belief; rather the classical tradition was seen as one element in divine revelation, so producing a syncretism which alarmed conservative churchmen.

By the mid 16th century the Italian renaissance was losing its impetus. The first unique burst of innovation could not be maintained. The Counter Reformation church now demanded a more orthodox treatment of subject matter, both in literature and in painting. Much great work continued to be done, particularly in the Veneto. Paladio used Roman models in creating the architectural style which would bear his name, while Titian and his contemporaries were laying the foundations of what would become the baroque style. Generations of artists and patrons continued to travel to Italy to absorb the culture both of its classical past and of the present.

The Northern Renaissance. Some of the great painters of the Flemish school crossed the Alps and were much admired by Renaissance artists. Perhaps because they were not surrounded by antiquities in their home environment, however, they never made the sharp break with the gothic. Italian styles took many years to become established north of the Alps.

Northern Europe's unique contribution came in the field of scholarship and literature. Here writers were free from the restrictions of the Counter Reformation and fear of the Inquisition. Protestants wanted to make the Bible available to all. The translations of the scriptures by Martin Luther and William Tyndale were immensely influential in formalizing the written forms of German and English respectively. Traditional interpretations of the Bible were challenged when Erasmus of Rotterdam produced a version of the New Testament in the original Greek. Latin was now ceasing to be the universal language of scholarship. While a return to the vernacular liberated learning from the cloisters of the church, it also fractured the international culture, which had reached its peak in the 12th century.

A strong secular tradition now flourished in England. Chaucer had already written for the newly educated merchant class. In 1510 John Colet, Dean of St. Paul's Cathedral and close friend of Erasmus, made a gesture to the secularisation of learning when he closed his cathedral school and re-founded it under the control of a trading guild. The combination of Tyndale's language and renaissance scholarship had created a uniquely favourable environment when in 1585 an actor called William Shakespeare left his native Stratford to chance his fortune in London.

The great flowering of French literature came in the 17th century. Corneille and Racine were still in essence renaissance writers, handling classical themes with a paladian sense of form and style.

Printing. Most importantly, the re-invention of printing by movable type provided the means of dissemination of both religious and secular literature. Whether the innovation be credited to Johannes Guttenberg of Maintz or Lourens Coster of Haarlem, the technique provided the means of dissemination of the works of any author. Books became cheaper as print runs grew longer. In the following centuries print was used to promote colonies, to circulate scurrilous pamphlets to produce works on magic – as well as to disseminate works of scholarship, religion and literature. In 1702 *The Courant*, the world's first daily newspaper, was published in London. Soon afterwards works of popular fiction began to come off the presses. Print had become an integral part of Western life.

The Advancement of Science.

The Copernican Revolution. In Hellenistic times the idea had been posited that the earth rotated round the sun, but this had not won general acceptance and in 16th century it was still generally accepted that the heavenly bodies rotated around a stationary earth. In 1543, however, the Polish scholar Copernicus published a book arguing the theory of heliocentric astronomy.

Copernicus' theory received little attention. During this time, however, Dutch craftsmen were experimenting with glass lenses. They made spectacles and also telescopes for use at sea. One of these telescopes fell into the hands of the Italian teacher, Galileo Galilei, and he turned the instrument towards the skies. By studying sun spots, the phases of Venus and the rings of Jupiter, he provided clear proof that Copernicus had been correct.

Galileo delayed publishing his findings because he recognized that they must arouse a storm of controversy. Authority, both of the Bible and of ancient authors clearly supported a geocentric universe, and the church still held to authority as the arbiter of truth. He published his findings in 1632, but, faced with the terror of the Inquisition, he recanted in 1633.

Descartes – The Turning Point. Tradition states that,

after formally accepting that the earth remained stationary, Galileo muttered 'it goes on moving'. Certainly the scientific impetus continued. In 1637 the French philosopher Descartes published *Discours de la Method*, which laid down what has become known as the Cartesian method. He argued that the experimental scientific process was the arbiter of truth. The pursuit of truth now involved breaking down knowledge into ever smaller areas of study. Medicine, for instance, became concerned with analysing the symptoms of disease in minute detail – arguably at the expense of a more integrated approach to the healing process.

In his dictum, *cogito ergo sum*, Descartes proclaimed the individualism which was to be the hallmark of modern European society. Western man had at last emerged from the shadow of past authorities, be they religious or classical. Personally a devout Catholic, Descartes rejected authority as an arbiter of faith and proclaimed that it had to be discovered through the human intellect. This was recognized as a fundamental challenge to the church, and Louis XIV personally ensured that Descartes was denied Christian burial.

Northern Europe. The condemnation of both Galileo and Descartes, and continued activities of the Inquisition placed scientists who lived in Catholic countries in an invidious position. In Protestant countries scientists might meet hostility from those who defended religious authority, but they did not face persecution. The impetus for scientific innovation therefore passed to Northern Europe.

The first protestant scientist was the German, Kepler, who provided information on the movements of planets. Dutch scientists, continuing their work with lenses, developed the microscope. This opened up whole new areas of study in such areas as the biological sciences. In England the cause of experimental science was argued by the Lord Chancellor, Francis Bacon, who had early visions of its potential. In 1619, William Harvey demonstrated the mechanism of the circulation of the blood.

The advances in navigation, first in Holland, and then in France and, above all, in England, drove forward skills in cartography and geographical study. Progress in astronomy and in the construction of clocks were spin-offs from this navigational programme. Landsmen could now own clocks and watches which told the time with great accuracy. People began to organize their lives around them, and to treat the hours and minutes of the day with a new respect.

The revolution started by Copernicus was completed by Isaac Newton, who published his *Principia Mathematica* in 1687. While Galileo argued the structure of the universe, Newton demonstrated the gravitational mechanism by which it worked. In the words of the poet Alexander Pope;

Nature and nature's laws lay hid in night:
God said, 'Let Newton be!' and all was light.

Until Newton's time, man was an uncomprehending plaything of fate or divine providence. Now he began to understand that the everyday events of life were driven by a structure of causation. Later generations of scientists have maintained the process. Mendel worked out the structure of genetic inheritance, Darwin illustrated the mechanism evolution, Pasteur demonstrated the causes of disease; Crick and Watson unravelled the DNA code. These and many other insights make up the intellectual baggage of Western man.

Enlightenment to Romanticism.

The Philosophes. The new enlightenment was to find its home in France, but the pattern of thinking owed much to 17th century British writers, notably John Locke, who published his *Essay Concerning Human Understanding* in 1690. Locke said that many religious issues were beyond human knowledge, and he argued for tolerance and reliance on reason and reasonableness. His work reflected a wide change of mood, singnalling the end of two centuries of religious strife; never again would the battle lines of Europe's terrible wars be drawn along religious lines.

The scientific advances of the 17th century encouraged philosophers of the following century to see the world as an ordered machine, much like one of the new clocks. There was an optimistic view that the universe was driven by a well oiled logic, and, if people could only behave in a reasonable manner, the world's problems could be readily overcome. Past religious passions now appeared irrelevant. Many thinkers no longer saw God as an imminent cause of good or evil, but as a great watch-maker, an ultimate mover, who no longer had immediate relevance to life. The poet Pope, himself a Catholic, again provided the aphorism of the age with the couplet;

> Know then thyself; presume not God to scan;
> The proper study of mankind is man.

The dominant personality among the *philosophes* was the Frenchman, Voltaire. He was a satirist, rather than an original thinker, and he turned his barbed pen on anything which he saw as repressive or pretentious. Voltaire had problems with the French authorities, but he and his circle sewed seeds of scepticism about the old order which would have immense repercussions in the later years of the century.

Evangelicalism. The first reaction against the intellectual emphasis of the age came with a religious revival, which developed in parallel in England and her North American colonies, both within and outside the Church of England. John Wesley set the emotional tone of the movement, sharply in contrast with the language of the *philosophes*, when he described how he 'felt his heart strangely warmed'. This new protestantism appealed primarily not to authority, but to the conversion experience. Until then, the Protestant churches had left missionary work almost entirely to the Catholic orders, but, by the end of the century, the worldwide tide of Protestant missions was beginning to flow, with incalculable, if often ambiguous, effects on non-European cultures.

Romanticism. If John Wesley represented the religious, Swiss born philosopher, Jean Jaques Rousseau, led the secular reaction against Cartesian intellectualism. He proclaimed that man was pure when in the simple state, be that the uncorrupted form of a noble savage, or a new born child. The quest for goodness therefore involved a return to nature. Rousseau, more than any other person, taught people to look on their environment as a place of beauty; since the time of Hannibal travellers had crossed the Alps, without pausing to recognize them as anything other than a barrier on the road to Italy. Now, as if overnight, Rousseau's Swiss mountains were discovered as majestic things of beauty.

As romanticism emphasised the emotions above the intellect, so it elevated the creative artist, as the person most able to express those emotions. The great milestones of the movement, such as Wordsworth and Coleridge's *Lyrical Balads*, Beethoven's *Eroica Sym-*

phony, the late paintings of Turner, explored new forms and emotions. This could lead to excess, but it also opened the way to the achievements, such as those of French impressionist painters and the great romantic composers.

Social Reform. At about the same time, first clearly surfacing in the 1770s, a transformation began to occur in attitudes to social issues. For centuries, Europeans had been shipping Africans to slavery with no apparent compunction. Now powerful anti-slavery movements made themselves heard in France, Denmark, England and other countries. Movements for the reform of vicious penal systems, the abolition of the 'hanging codes' and for the humane treatment of the insane can be dated to the same time. Educational reform also became a cause for the future.

Credit for this new mood of social reform has been given to the pen of Voltaire, the preaching of Wesley and the ideals of Rousseau. All played their part. In education, for instance, evangelical passion to bring truth to the poor led directly to the opening of ragged schools, while Rousseau was laying the foundations for the quite separate development of child centred learning, which was carried forward by the Swiss educator, Pestalozzi. The cause of reform was uniquely in the air and the traditional political structures were ill equipped to contain it. Europe was ready for the cataclysm of the French Revolution.

8. Revolution.

The French Revolution.

The Estates General. In 1776 the British government was faced with a major revolution in its American colonies (Chapter 11). King Louis XVI of France, recognizing this as an opportunity of regaining some of the ground lost in the Seven Years War, involved France in the conflict. In military terms the intervention was successful; in financial terms it was a disaster. The French government, always in financial straits, was now unable to function. The shortfall could no longer be met by the time honoured device of increasing taxes on the poor, but those able to pay could only be taxed with their own consent. Members of the aristocracy recognized an opportunity of winning concessions from the monarchy in return for money, and they insisted that Louis should recall the French parliament, the *Estates General*, which had not met for 150 years.

The body met in three separate houses – aristocracy, clergy and the third estate. This last house represented the property owning middle classes and was largely made up of professional men. They had no vision of themselves as revolutionaries, but they were influenced by the ideas of the *philosophes* and of the American Declaration of Independence. Louis anticipated doing his business with the other two houses before disbanding the body, but the Third Estate had equal representation with the other two, and could count on considerable support in the House of Clergy. In the summer of 1789 the Third Estate declared that it constituted a National Assembly. Louis gave way before its demands and the body set about a huge programme of constitutional, administrative and social reform.

Popular Unrest. Since the time of the Frondes, French kings had been acutely aware of the dangers of uprisings among the poor, who remained unrepresented in the National Assembly. There was unrest in many parts of the countryside, where chateaux were attacked and hated rent books burned. The most immediate danger, however, came from the poor of Paris, who found themselves caught in a spiral of inflation, most crucially in the price of bread. By the 14th July, it was estimated that only three days supply remained in the storehouses of the capital.

The mob possessed armaments, but little ammunition. This lay under close guard in the royal castle of the Bastille. On the 14th July the mob stormed the Bastille, leaving Louis quite helpless. He could not use his army because the loyalty of rank and file soldiers was in doubt. Many of the aristocracy were now fleeing France and in June 1791 Louis and his family made their bid to escape. They were captured and brought back as prisoners to the capital. The Assembly maintained the King as a figurehead until he and signed the new Constitution in September. The body disbanded itself to make way for the new Legislative Assembly.

War and the Terror. Since the National Assembly had barred any of their number from seeking re- election, the new body was made up of inexperienced men. The dominant figures were Danton, who surrounded himself with members from the Gironde, in southern France, and the little lawyer Robespierre, whose power was based on the Jacobin Club. Protagonists of the new order now felt under siege. The King could still serve as a focal point for a royalist counter-revolution, and both Austria and Prussia were issuing threats. Robespierre argued that peace should be preserved, but Danton believed that the nation could only be united by war. He urged his fellow countrymen to 'dare and dare and dare again' and Frenchmen responded to his cry that the *patrie* was in danger. In April 1792, France declared war on Austria, and Prussia came in on the side of Austria. Early news from the war was disastrous and the capital was gripped in a fever. On the 30th July a contingent marched into the capital, singing the song which would become the national anthem. They demanded that Louis should be dethroned and a republic proclaimed. The men of Marseilles were soon joined by a huge citizen army which, chanting the Marseillaise, threw itself on and routed the mercenary enemy soldiers at Valmy on the 20th September. Two days later, France was declared a republic. Louis was placed on trial in December and executed on the 21st January 1793.

The citizen's army swept across the Netherlands and at last achieved the 'natural frontiers' which had been beyond the reach of the armies of Louis XIV. The victors proclaimed liberty and equality for the poor of all lands, but in practice all too often they laid new tax burdens on those same poor to pay the cost of war.

In February 1793 France faced a coalition of Britain, Austria, Prussia, Holland, Spain, Sardinia and Italian states. Action taken against the Catholic church also provoked civil war in the conservative regions of the Vendée and Brittany. Effective power now passed from the Assembly to a Committee of Public Safety. In June, Danton's Gironde fell to Robespierre's Jacobins and the period, known as the Reign of Terror, began. Among the victims were successive waves of politicians, including both Danton and his Girondins and Robespierre and the Jacobins. As a result, power passed to a new generation of second rate men, who could not command the respect of the nation.

Meanwhile, the French citizen army, now reinforced by the first use of conscription in modern times, was more than holding its own in the war. Britain, while formidable at sea, was poorly equipped for a land war and the old enemies, Prussia and Austria, failed to co-ordinate their effort. The French armies, now led by a new generation of generals, remained firmly entrenched on the Rhine.

The Empire.

The rise of Napoleon. In May 1798 a French army, led by the Corsican Napoleon Bonaparte, was sent to invade Egypt in an attempt to cut British trade routes. Land victories were made worthless when the British fleet, commanded by Admiral Nelson, destroyed the French supply fleet, and so cut the army off from Europe. In August 1899 Napoleon abandoned his army and returned to France to challenge the discredited leaders of the nation. His gambler's throw succeeded and on November 9th he staged a coup d'etat and assumed the title of First Consul. He set about centralizing power in his own hands; in 1802 he became consul for life, and in 1804, he followed the example of Charlemagne by crowning himself Emperor as Napoleon I. Any dismay at his negation of the ideals of the revolution was overwhelmed by the relief of ordinary Frenchmen at the return of ordered and firm government.

153

Imperial Government. Napoleon had a genius fo
administration. After an initial purge of remainin
Jacobins, he set about healing old divisions and re
uniting the country. He recognized that the continuin
civil war in the Vendée could not be brought to an en
unless the state came to terms with the Catholic churcl
so the old religion was restored to its position as th
national faith. He set about recruiting the ablest men int
government, regardless of whether they held republica
or royalist sympathies. Most enduringly, he personall
supervised a detailed revision of the whole of the Frenc
legal system into the *Code Napoleon.* Had Napoleo
been content to hold the Rhine frontier and bring soun
administration to France, his rule could have been ou
standingly successful. But he was by instinct a genera
and the symbolic identification with Charlemagne at hi
coronation illustrated his determination to build th
greatest empire that the world had seen. 'I am destined t
change the face of the world. ' he declared. But Napc
leon, like Louis XVI, discovered that wars could only b
fought at a financial cost, which had to be passed on i
taxes to the ordinary people of France and the conquere
countries.

The Napoleonic Wars. The great struggles of prev
ous centuries had achieved little more than change th
line of a frontier here and there. In the three years fror
1805 Napoleon completely redrew the map of Europe

He owed his success to the army which he had inherited from the revolution. Opposing generals recognized that the citizens' armies of France were carried forward on a tide of national energy, which had been released by the revolution. Napoleon added to this a military professionalism, identified with the magnificent Imperial Guard. The surge of victories carried the army across Europe as far as Bohemia, north into Scandinavia and south into Italy and Spain. Ancient rulers were replaced by members of the Bonaparte family or generals from the army. Even then, however, Britain, Spain and Russia remained as weak points remained in the French Continental System.

Giving priority to the invasion of Britain, Napoleon gathered barges at the channel ports. Any hope of carrying out this operation, however, ended in 1805 when the French fleet was destroyed at the Battle of Trafalgar. Britain therefore remained an implacable foe across the Channel.

The victorious French army in Spain found itself unable to overcome a fierce guerilla resistance which made full use of the broken terrain. The British despatched a force under the general who would later become the Duke of Wellington. In August 1812, after a relentless campaign, Wellington led his army into Madrid.

As Madrid fell, Napoleon was on the other side of

Europe, leading 450,000 men on his disastrous campaign against Russia. He had already heavily defeated the Russian army and he believed that serfs would flock to join him once they heard that he had proclaimed their emancipation. He defeated the Russian army again at Borodino and marched on across the scorched countryside to occupy Moscow. But, when the Russians burned their own capital city around his army, and winter began to set in, he was forced to order the terrible retreat. In the end, only a tenth of his great army survived the ordeal. The Imperial Guard was reduced to some 400 men; 80,000 horses had died, leaving the emperor with no effective cavalry to put in the field.

Defeats in Spain and Russia shattered the myth of invincibility and by 1814 Napoleon had lost everything. Paris fell on the 30th March and he abdicated his imperial crown on the 11th April. In France, however, loyalty to the deposed emperor remained strong and, when he escaped from exile in 1815, men flocked to join his army. The hundred days adventure ended when he was defeated by the combined British and Prussian armies at Waterloo on the 18th June.

Napoleon passed the remainder of his life in well guarded exile, but the Napoleonic legend lived on. As French power declined, people remembered that it was the Little Corporal who had led them to glory.

Reaction and Revolution.

The Return of the Old Order. After the defeat of Napoleon, members of the old ruling houses moved back into their palaces. The statesmen met in Vienna to reorganize the continent. The treaty took little account of nationalist aspirations. Poland was awarded to Russia; Venice and Lombardy to Austria; the Rhineland was taken from France and given to Prussia; the southern Netherlands were incorporated into Holland; Norway was made a part of Sweden.

The Austrian Prince Metternich was the main architect of this restoration of the old order. He fully recognized the huge changes in political consciousness brought about by the French Revolution, but he believed that these had to be suppressed, and that structures should return to return to their dynastic roots. He opposed all representative institutions, and established the Holy League as a coalition of powers dedicated to suppress ideas of liberty and nationalism, wherever they might show themselves. Of the major powers, only Britain - itself, however imperfectly, a representative government – stood apart to uphold a more liberal tradition.

The policy of intervention was successfully invoked when the Spanish people rose in rebellion in 1820. Austria also put down rebellion in her Italian possessions. Metternich was wise enough to see himself as the defender of a dying way of life. In 1821 the people of

Greece rose against their Turkish masters. True to his principles, Metternich gave Austrian support to the Ottoman Turks, but the rebels won backing from Russia and Britain and achieved their independence in 1830.

Also in 1830 the people of Paris rose again and replaced the conservative king with his more liberal cousin, Louis Philippe and revolutions broke out in Poland and across Germany. In the same year, the Catholic Belgians rebelled against their Dutch masters. The conservative powers threatened to intervene, but Britain, in a gesture which would be called in 84 years later, guaranteed Belgian independence.

The Year of Revolutions. The unrest of 1830 was a prelude to much greater upheavals of 1848. In January, rebellion broke out in Sicily. In February the people of Paris drove Louis Philippe, now a figure of fun, into exile. In March, Venice, Parma, Milan and Sardinia all rose against Austria. As the year progressed, there was revolution in Poland and Hungary. Smaller German princes fell, most never to return. Uprisings in Berlin and Vienna even brought the powerful Prussian and Austrian states to the point of collapse, and the elderly Metternich had to follow Louis Philippe into exile.

The Hughes Capet French monarchy was finished for ever, and, after a period of civil war the French people turned again to the magic name of Napoleon, in the person of his nephew, Louis Napoleon. He followed family tradition by staging a coup d'état and assuming the title of Emperor Napoleon III. Across the rest of Europe, the ruling houses re-established control over their dominions.

New Nations.

The Unification of Italy. A decade later, Camillo Cavour, a statesman in the Italian kingdom of Savoy, set about achieving by political means what had been beyond the powers of the revolutionaries. In 1858 he met with Napoleon III to discuss how Austrian rule might be ended and Italy unified under his King, Victor Emmanuel of Savoy. In 1859 French armies inflicted heavy defeats on the Austrians at Magenta and Solferino. In 1860, the popular soldier Garibaldi led 'the thousand' against the rulers of Sicily and Naples. He handed these territories over to Victor Emmanuel. For a time Austria held on to Venice, but the city fell in 1866. Finally the Papal States were brought into a united Italy in 1870. The political task was complete, but the new country faced formidable problems of poverty, and large numbers, particularly from the south, emigrated to find a better life.

The Unification of Germany. In 1862 Otto von Bismark, a nobleman of Junker descent, became Prime Minister of Prussia. His first speech was ominous for the future of European peace. 'The great issues of our day can not be solved by speeches and majority votes – but by blood and iron. ' The German speaking people were already showing a formidable potential, but to achieve all they had to be united into a nation state. Only Austria or Prussia could be the focus of that state; Bismark determined that it should be Prussia.

In 1864 the two powers collaborated to annex the German speaking lands of Schleswig and Holstein from Denmark. Then two years later Prussia went to war with Austria. On the 3rd July 1866 the Hapsburg army was devastatingly defeated at Sadowa. The Hapsburg monarchy retained Austria, but Germany was now effectively united. In 1870 Germany went to war with France and the Napoleonic legend was laid for ever on the field of Sedan.

As Bismark's army occupied Paris, there could no longer be any doubt that Germany was the dominant power in continental Europe. The violent methods by which this had been achieved were no innovation in European politics. The new state was based on admirable organization. German cities were models of organization and sanitary efficiency; a state school place was provided for every child, and illiteracy rates became the lowest in the world; the poor, who until that time had emigrated in large numbers, now showed their confidence in the government of their country by staying at home, and by playing their part in constructing the impressive industrial base of the new nation.

9. A Changing World.

The Infrastructure of Change.

Population. The population of Europe had been growing relentlessly since the time of the Black Death. Demographers have argued why, for instance, the increase was particularly pronounced in the 16th century. It appears as though women started marrying younger, so having a longer child bearing life, but this leaves unanswered why such a social change should have occurred. The 18th century again saw a steady increase across western Europe, which pre-dated major medical advances of the following century. A modest alleviation of the harsh conditions of rural life, the improvement of the housing stock, and some advances in public health may all have contributed to a reduction in the death rate.

Rulers generally welcomed a rising population; it provided an larger man-power pool for the military, and increased the tax base of the nation. In 1798, however, an English clergyman, called Thomas Malthus, published his *Essay on Population.* The world, he argued, possesses limited resources. As population grows, so the most vulnerable – the poor – must inevitably experience disaster and hunger. Malthus' work was influential, but his warnings were not, in the short term, authenticated by events. The reason for this was that, at the same time that the population was increasing, Europe was experiencing a green revolution, which greatly increased the amount of food available to meet the growing demand.

The Second Agricultural Revolution. The first great change in farming practice came with the introduction of settled agriculture at the beginning of historical times (Chapter 1). Even in Babylonian cities, farming families had to produce a surplus to feed craftsmen, priests and warriors. By the beginning of the 18th century, little had changed. It is estimated that in England eight out of ten people still lived in the countryside and that, on average, one farming family had to keep one other family from the produce of its land. People still ate bread baked from their own wheat and drank beer brewed from their own barley. Animals, except for breeding stock were still slaughtered and salted down for the winter.

Once again, change originated in small, highly ur-banized, 17th century Holland. Dutch farms had to be more efficient than those of their larger neighbours, and major improvements were pioneered, particularly in the development of root vegetables, largely for animal win-ter feed, and in high yield artificial grasses, such as alfalfa and lucerne.

In the 18th century, the English gentry, unlike their neighbours in France, lived on their estates and it became fashionable to take an interest in farming. George III set the tone by contributing articles to a farming journal. Some began to introduce the Dutch innovations on their estates. New crops and methods of rotation were introduced and selective breeding produced remarkable improvements in the quality of livestock.

These improvements could not be introduced without radical changes in the organization of the countryside. Improved agriculture could not be successfully introduced in the old communal fields, so enclosures, which had been taking place for two centuries, were given a new impetus. In the change from peasant holdings to larger farms, worked by landless labourers, many lost land and ancient rights. The production of food, however, became a much more efficient process. By the late 18th century British farmers were in a position to support a huge increase in the nation's urban population.

Financial and Human Resources. Any major economic expansion needs to be built on a sound financial base. Britain's growing international trade brought prosperity, and her island position meant that wealth did not have to be dissipated on the maintenance of a large standing army. By the standards of the time, she also had a sophisticated and well capitalised banking industry.

It is harder to establish a link between the skills

required for technological advance and the social and educational structure of the day. Few of the innovators of the new age came form the conventional academic background, which had produced Isaac Newton; they were more typically self taught, or the products of Scottish or dissenting education.

Economic Theory. In 1776 Adam Smith published *The Wealth of Nations*, which laid the basis of modern economics. He argued the benefits of competition in a free economy, against both state control and the abuses of monopoly powers. His arguments were influential both in government and business circles, initially in Britain and later in the United States and elsewhere.

The First Industrial Revolution.

Iron and Coal. Since the time of the Hittites, iron working had been centred on the great forests. The charcoal used in the smelting process consumed large quantities of timber, which was also vital for building and naval supplies. Over the centuries, the forests receded to the more remote areas. By the end of the 17th century, Britain faced something of a crisis. In the 14th century, German craftsmen of the Rhineland had learnt how to make cast iron, so that the metal could now be used to make a wider range of products, but there was an acute shortage of wood to drive the blast furnaces.

Early in the 18th century the Darby family of Shropshire finally solved the problem of how iron could be smelted from coal. As this technique became widely known, industry moved from the forests to the great coal fields, which lie across Europe in a band from mid Russia to Wales. Surface coal was soon exhausted and deep mines were sunk to exploit the seams. Iron goods could now be produced in bulk.

Steam Power. As early as Hellenistic times, it had been recognized in theory that steam could be used to drive an engine, but the technological basis was lacking. The need for pumps to drain the new deep mines made progress all the more essential. The Scottish engineer, James Watt made the essential break-through when he separated the cylinder from the condenser. As a result, industry could now be liberated, not only from the forests, but also from the banks of fast flowing rivers.

Water Transport. Before the 18th century, land transport was rudimentary over most of Europe. Once again, the Dutch had pioneered the use of the canals which drained their country for transporting loads. The French government also constructed the magnificent Canal du Midi, designed to prevent goods having to be carried around the coast of Spain. France also had a high quality road network, built by forced labour, but these, like those of the Romans, were built for military use.

In 1861 the Duke of Bridgewater opened a canal which linked his coal mine at Worsley with the growing town of Manchester. The potential for improved communications to lubricate economic growth was illustrated when the price of coal in Manchester fell immediately by a half. The great revolution occurred, however, when steam power was applied to locomotion. Here the initiative was taken in the United States, where inland waterways provided the essential communication links for the new nation. In 1807, Robert Fulton sailed *The Steamboat* from New York to Albany in 32 hours – a journey which had previously taken four days. Two years later, steam power was applied to ocean navigation.

Railways. The world's first commercial railway was opened in Britain in 1825, between Stockton and Darlington. Huge sums of money were invested in railway building in many nations, but, despite massive construction programmes, especially in the United States and Germany, Britain retained her initial advantage. The age of cheap and rapid communication brought important social as well as economic change, as the structure of society began to reflect the new mobility.

Cotton and the Factory System. There had long been a market for fine fabrics in western Europe. By the early 18th century a substantial silk industry had grown up in France, which reduced dependence on imports. At this time, cotton was still a luxury fabric, and ready woven cloth was imported from India. Entrepreneurs then began to import raw cotton, which was put out for manufacture to domestic workers. Whole families worked immensely long hours at carding, spinning and weaving to earn a modest subsistence. The early machines were invented by enterprising craftsmen to help boost domestic output.

The first large spinning factory was built by Richard Arkwright at Cromford, near Derby in 1771. By the early 19th century all the stages of cotton cloth production had been brought within the factory system. Britain, backed by her huge merchant marine, had established a dominant position in the world supply of textiles. One machine, tended by a woman or a girl, could now do the work of many domestic workers, and traditional producers, from Britain itself to India, lost their livelihood.

Despite being a closely guarded secret, the new technology was bound to become known. The United States was already showing itself a fertile ground for industrial development and a substantial industry grew up in New England.

Urban Growth. The population of Europe continued to grow rapidly throughout the 19th century, but the increase was now concentrated in the urban centres. In the 19th century, the population of London increased from about 900,000 to some 4.7 million, that of Paris from 600,000 to 3.6 million; small country towns turned into conurbations. This growth in Europe was matched by comparable expansion of New York and the midwestern cities of the United States.

The urban centres grew faster than their service infrastructure, and so the industrial revolution became identified with slum housing, malnutrition and cholera, on a scale which remains common in the burgeoning cities of modern developing countries. For most of the workers, however, the change from rural to urban poverty was not the disaster that has often been painted. The poor had always lived on the edge of subsistence; there were indeed reverses, as during the 'hungry forties', but the overall tendency was towards an improvement in living standards. Pasteur's discovery of the germ causation of disease stimulated major sewage and other sanitation projects in the second half of the century.

The Second Industrial Revolution.

The Decline of Britain. Visitors to the Great Exhibition, which was held in London in 1851, would not have readily recognized that the age of British industrial supremacy was already nearing its end. Britain possessed half of the world's mileage of railway lines, and half of its merchant marine. Five years later, the British inventor, Henry Bessemer would present his Convertor, which made possible the mass production of steel. The nation's lead still appeared unassailable.

In hindsight it is, however, possible to recognize the signs of decay. Too much investment lay in the industries of the first industrial revolution, which were vulnerable to competition from low cost countries; the educational system, both for the rich and poor was ill equipped to train in the more technical skills needed to meet the ever growing complexities of industry; British industry was already at times failing to capitalize on the skills of the inventors.

Germany and the United States. In the second half of the century two powers demonstrated great economic potential. German military expenditure funded the expansion of the mighty firm of Alfred Krupp, which was soon competing with British companies for the supply of railway and shipyard equipment. The electric dynamo was invented simultaneously in Britain and Germany, but the German firm of Siemens reaped the benefits. In 1885 Carl Benz produced the first working automobile using the internal combustion engine, so initiating the greatest transport revolution in the world's history.

The United States was also showing both creativity and economic power. Inventive geniuses, like Bell and Edison, found that the young nation, with its growing market base, provided an ideal environment for the exploitation of new technology. The telegraph, the telephone, the domestic sewing machine, mechanised agricultural machines, the safety lift, air conditioning, the electric light, the phonograph, the cine camera and the aeroplane were all American contributions to the more sophisticated second phase of industrialisation. Andrew Carnegie and Henry Ford also showed the American capacity to build great operations on the inventions of others.

Capital and Labour.

Trades Unions. Throughout history, there had always been a sharp divide between the rich and the poor, but the working people within the new factory system became acutely aware of the polarization between those who owned the means of production and their employees. By gathering workers together in large units of production, the owners made it practicable for them to organize in defence of their living conditions.

Robert Owen, a working man, turned successful cotton master, attempted to establish a model industrial society at New Lanark, Scotland; he introduced schools and all kinds of leisure activities for the working people, and still was able to show a profit for the mill. He became dissatisfied with this paternalistic approach and set up a co-operative venture in New Harmony in America. This proved less successful, and he returned to Britain, where he founded the ambitious Grand National Consolidated Trades Union. This was a bid to harness the power of the working people, so that they could control the industries in which they worked. Owen's union failed, as did most of the early attempts to organize labour. Unskilled workers, faced by organized management, lacked credible bargaining power. Over much of Europe, they were further weakened by being divided between opposing Christian and socialist unions.

The battle between capital and labour could be seen in its rawest state in the United States. The owners mobilized city and state authorities and hired private armies to break strikes. Also there were as yet no anti-trust laws to prevent employers from combining to achieve their objectives. The workers responded by organizing themselves into violent secret societies, like the Molly Macguires of the Pennsylvania coal mines. At Andrew Carnegie's Homestead works at Pittsburgh in 1892, the two sides confronted each other in pitched battle.

At Homestead, as elsewhere, management emerged victorious because there was always unskilled 'blackleg' labour on hand to fill the jobs of those who went on strike. At the end of the century, however, there emerged a new generation of union leaders who recognized that progress could best be made by organizing the skilled labour, which was now vital for the more sophisticated industries. In The United States, in 1886, Samuel Gompers organized these skilled trades into the more successful American Federation of Labour. In the years which followed, the rights of organized labour were increasingly recognized by the legal systems of the industrialised nations.

Socialism. During the time that Robert Owen was experimenting with new structures, continental thinkers were beginning to challenge the laissez-faire theories of Adam Smith. Most influential was the French nobleman, Claude de Saint-Simon, often looked on as the founder of socialism, who published his critique of the new industrial age in the 1820s. He argued for the replacement of the existing ruling elite by a 'meritocracy', which would manage the economy for the general good of the population, rather than for individual gain.

Saint-Simon's ideas gained ground in France. In 1848 Paris experienced two distinct revolutions. The first unseated the king; the second was a bloody confrontation between workers, proclaiming the new socialists ideas, and the bourgeoisie, who defended traditional property rights.

Communism. Karl Marx watched the destruction of the Paris workers in 1848 with distress but without surprise. He had been associated with the revolutionary movement in his native Germany before being forced into exile. He believed that history showed two struggles. The first, as in all earlier revolutions, had been between the feudal authorities and the bourgeoisie. The second, in his own day, lay between the bourgeoisie and the proletariat.

Marx held that the value of goods lay in the labour which had been expended in its production, and the interests of the proletariat lay in winning a fair return for that labour. That was in conflict with the interests of the owners, or bourgeoisie, who were dedicated to achieving a profit on the product. Within a capitalist society the proletariat was therefore alienated from the production process, and both sides were inevitably locked in class war. The objective for the proletariat was to win control of the machinery of government by revolution, and then to use the new communist state to control the 'commanding heights of the economy' – land, transport, factories and banks.

Marx and his friends tried to gather the revolutionary movement into the unity without which he believed it could never be effective. In 1864 the First International of the Communist party was held in London, with delegations from France, Germany, Italy, Switzerland and Poland, as well as Britain. The party, however, early showed its capacity for splitting into factions. When, by the beginning of the next century, none of the great industrial nations had fallen, many thought that the communist challenge had passed away. It was not anticipated that the revolution would come in Russia which, under Marx's definition, still lay within the feudal stage of development.

Change and Society.

Education. The movement for educational reform

can be traced to the late 18th century, but another century
had to pass before change affected the lives of working
people. In Germany and the United States, and later in
Japan, politicians recognized that, if a nation were to
remain competitive in the new world, it needed an
educated labour force. All across the industrial world
there was a huge increase, not only in basic education but
in the provision of higher education. Literacy and nu-
meracy were at last seen as functional skills, rather than
as the prerogative of a privileged elite.

The Women's Movement. Before the middle of the
19th century individual voices had been raised to protest
against the subjugation of women in western society, but
the origin of a formal movement can be placed in 1848,
the year of revolutions. In that year a group of women,
with men supporters, met at Seneca Falls in New York
State and laid out a programme which was to be the
blueprint for the women's movement. The resolutions
demanded voting rights, equality before the law, the right
to hold property, justice in marriage, equal opportunity in
education, free access to jobs and an end to the pervasive
double standard in morality. The political struggle became identified with the names of Susan Anthony in the
U. S. A. and later with the Pankhurst family in Britain.
Many advances were made, particularly in educational
provision, but the radical change came with World War
One. Women who undertook a wide range of men's work

174

could no longer be denied basic rights.

Leisure. Towards the end of the century working hours began to be reduced and, perhaps for the first time in history, the less privileged found themselves with time for leisure activities. Virtually all the major sports, which are popular across the world today, were codified during these decades, and this happened mainly in Britain, where the industrial achievements brought the earliest benefits. By the beginning of the 20th century, the bicycle and the railway excursion were giving urban dwellers a new sense of freedom. Many problems remained, but those who lived in the industrial societies experienced a genuine improvement in the quality of life. This improvement made the programmes of the revolutionaries less attractive than Karl Marx and his followers had anticipated.

10. America

The Birth of the United States.

The Causes of Conflict. When the Seven Years War ended in 1763 it appeared that Britain had achieved her aims in the New World. The French colonies in Canada had fallen under British rule and the stranglehold on the Thirteen Colonies by French forts on the Ohio River had been broken. Very shortly, however, it became clear that strains were building up in the relationships between the American colonists and the mother country.

Under the mercantilist system, it was taken for granted that the colonies existed for the benefit of the other country. As American economies strengthened, however, they began to generate their own momentum. Slaving ships from New England, for instance, now competed directly with those from Bristol on the Guinea Coast.

The American colonists had already developed the westward momentum, which remains a feature of the nation today. Pioneers were penetrating into the rich lands to the west of the Appalachians. Britain, as the colonizing power, was responsible for security, and the London government therefore had to decide whether to expand budgets to provide protection to these pioneers. To the annoyance of many colonists, a decision was taken that a limit should be drawn along the ridge of the Appalachians. The government further decided that the American colonies should be taxed to help pay security costs. When the traditional colonial assemblies refused to vote the funds, the British government decided to establish the principle of its right to impose direct taxation. The Stamp Act, the Sugar Act and the duty on tea were all stages in the deteriorating relationships. None were in themselves onerous, but they created genuine anxiety. Sugar molasses, for instance, was turned into rum which was the staple of the slave trade. Any tax could be used to make American ships uncompetitive with their British rivals.

Independence. Tension centred on the largest city and trading port of Boston, where fighting started in 1775. In the following year representatives from the Thirteen colonies, now to become states, met in Philadelphia to declare themselves independent. The famous and highly influential Declaration of Independence, drafted by Thomas Jefferson, justified the act of rebellion in terms which drew from Locke and the *philosophes*. It declared that government derives from the consent of the governed and the misgovernment, listed in detail, broke that tie of consent.

The colonists faced serious problems in organizing themselves to fight a major European power; there was little natural unity, and money to fund the conflict proved as hard to raise as it had been under British rule. American success was largely the result of the outstanding leadership qualities of George Washington and the ability of the colonists to adapt to a guerilla style of warfare, well suited to the heavily forested terrain. In 1781, the British army surrendered at Yorktown and two years later, Britain accepted defeat.

The Constitution. It was not immediately clear, however, whether one or thirteen new nations had emerged from the conflict. Many of Washington's army remained unpaid and no mechanism existed for a central government to raise money from the states. The Constitutional Convention of 1787 was faced with serious division between the interests of large and of small states, and between those who wanted to see a strong central government and those who preferred to see real power continue to lie with the individual states. The final document, which was ratified in 1788, steered a compromise course between the interests. The Executive, Legislature and Judiciary all had their own spheres of responsibility, and acted as a control on one another by a complex structure of checks and balances.

Canada.

The successful rebellion by the American colonies left the British government reluctant to expend further effort and resources on colonization. Many loyalists from the south had moved north, and the division between the French and English population remained deep. The colonies covered much sparsely populated territory and communications remained poor. The people were united only in a common hostility to any threat of annexation by the more powerful neighbour to the south.

In the first half of the 19th century, progress was made towards the establishment of a confederacy. In 1867 The British North America Act brought together four provinces into a federal Dominion of Canada. To protect minority French interests, language and education remained provincial concerns and other provinces joined the federation in subsequent years. In 1885 the last rivet was driven into the Canadian Pacific Line, bringing together east and west and opening up the prairies for agricultural development.

Latin America.

To the south, the countries of Latin America remained under the colonial control of Spain and Portugal. The successful rebellion of the British colonies was shortly followed by the collapse of the old monarchies in the face of Napoleon's army. Links with the old countries were cut during the European wars, and this generated an outburst of nationalist fervour.

Spain fought a series of devastating wars to recover control of her American empire. In 1810, the Mexican priest Manuel Hidalgo y Costilla led the poor in a rising, but independence was not finally won until 1821. Power then passed, not to the poor, but to the wealthy classes of Spanish descent. Rulers like Santa Anna treated the country as a personal *hacienda*, and the situation of the poor became, if anything, worse than it had been in colonial days.

In 1811 Venezuela declared its independence under the 'Great Liberator', Simon Bolivar. He had travelled in Europe and was particularly influenced by the writings of Voltaire, and he now saw himself as the George Washington who would bring unity to the Spanish speaking countries of South America. He won a series of victories against Spain and independence seemed assured, provided the conservative European powers did not follow Metternich's plan and intervene to uphold the old order. This was prevented by American President Monroe, who warned off any intervention by proclaiming his doctrine of 'hands off America'.

Bolivar seemed on the verge of creating a United Republic of Columbia, which could be a comparable power to the U. S. A. He was, however, unable to hold the new country together, and one part of the country after another broke off to form new nations. As in Mexico, the privileged classes preserved power to themselves. The European nations competed to invest, particularly in Argentina, and there was a steady stream of immigration from the Old World, but the old inequalities remained, and the economies of many of the new Latin American countries became dangerously dependant on single primary products.

The path to independence was smoother in Brazil. The Portuguese royal family decided not to defend its rights, and in 1822 the country was declared an independent empire by consent. Here too old social inequalities remained and, as late as 1888, Brazil was the last American country to abolish the Atlantic slave trade.

Slavery and the Civil War.

King Cotton. Dr. Samuel Johnson spoke for many when he poured scorn on American ideals of liberty, which were denied to the black slave population. The continuance of the institution was one of the issues discussed in the Constitutional Convention. There were three broad points of view. Opponents of slavery wished to see the institution outlawed in the new nation; representatives of the southern states would not contemplate joining a union which deprived them of their property; moderates, like Washington himself, opposed slavery, but they believed that they could let history take its course. Slavery, they argued, was outdated and it would wither away of its own accord. Events proved them wrong.

The new English cotton mills created an insatiable demand for raw cotton. The native short staple cotton was an uneconomic crop until in 1793 Eli Whitney invented a gin, which enabled it to be cleaned in large quantities. In the decades which followed huge areas of the south was given over to cotton cultivation. This created a demand for slaves. The Atlantic slave trade was declared illegal, but many were smuggled into the country; others were 'sold down the river' by plantation owners from the more northerly slave states.

This resurgence of slavery led to widespread unrest. Slave risings broke out and an increasing number of slaves used the freedom road to escape north. White and black activists combined in a highly organized anti-slavery movement. Anger rose when in 1850 Congress passed the Fugitive Slave Law, which gave southern owners the right to pursue their property into the free northern states.

Slave and Free States. The House of Representatives, elected by population, was dominated by the free states. The Senate was more finely balanced. As new states were added to the Union, the balance was maintained. California and Oregon tilted the balance towards the free states. 'Bleeding' Kansas, a fierce bone of contention, fell to the slave party. When, in 1860, a republican from Illinois called Abraham Lincoln was elected president, the slave states felt that the political balance had swung irretrievably against them. In March 1861 eleven southern states declared their secession from the Union and the following month they attacked the federal Fort Sumter. *The Civil War.* Over 600,000 men died in the four years of war which followed. The southern armies were highly motivated and generally well commanded, but they were bound to lose a long war of attrition. The industrial north had a larger population, more industrial production and more miles of railway. This was the first major war in history fought with armaments which were the products of the industrial revolution, and great battles, like Antietam and Gettysburg presaged the terrible loss of life at Verdun and on the Somme half a century later. When the war ended in April 1865, the south lay devastated. Lincoln was assassinated five days later.

Civil Rights. The war had been fought over the right of the south to secede from the Union. Slavery was abolished in the process. Lincoln's emancipation decree was given the force of law by the Thirteenth Amendment of 1865 and further amendments wrote civil rights into the constitution. In the years of reconstruction black legislators took their seats and it appeared as though political and social equality might be close. Gradually, however, by a process of manipulation and terrorisation, the white supremacists regained control of the southern states. The liberal fervour of the anti-slavery years was now spent, and the Supreme Court proved unwilling to uphold even most clearly defined constitutional rights. Disillusioned, many blacks migrated to the booming industrial cities of the north, where they encountered new forms of discrimination.

The situation only began to improve with the great Civil Rights movement of the 1960s, when Dr. Martin Luther King provided a rallying point for his people's aspirations and liberal white sympathizers were again mobilized, as they had been a century before in the anti-slavery campaign.

The Westward Movement.

Thomas Jefferson. Of all the founding fathers, Jefferson had the clearest vision that the new nation could become a great power, and that this had to be based on an exploitation of the great potential of the continent. He was the architect of the system whereby new states could be added to the Union. By 1803 Napoleon had decided that the Mississippi lands of Louisiana, which remained French, were of no value and Jefferson, now president, negotiated to buy them for $15,000,000 – and so double the land area of the United States. In 1804 he sent out an expedition led by Lewis and Clark to cross the continent and report back on its potential.

Jefferson's vision of the west as the land of opportunity gradually captured the American imagination. It was argued that the American people – by which was meant the white American people – had a 'manifest destiny' to possess the continent from the Atlantic to the Pacific Oceans.

The Dispossession of the Indian People. During the early years of the 19th century, Americans of European origin were pushing into traditional Indian territory beyond the Appalachians. Every expedient was used, from purchase to forced expulsion, to drive the Indian people back into the western grasslands, which remained unattractive to white settlement.

The nomadic buffalo culture of the plains Indians was based on horses originally acquired form the southern Spanish settlements, and it was therefore a comparatively recent development. In the middle of the century, migrants were attracted, not to the featureless plains with their extremes of climate, but to the far west. For a brief period, wagon trains and nomadic Indians were able to co-exist. By the 1870s, however, the white men began to move into these last hunting grounds. The buffalo were hunted to deprive the Indian people of their livlihood and provide food for railway construction workers; then the railway link with the eastern markets made the grasslands attractive for cattle farming. Finally new agricultural machinery and irrigation techniques made large scale wheat farming economic. With the buffalo herds destroyed, and their whole way of life undermined, the surviving Indian people were driven back into ever more arid and infertile reservations.

Oregon Country. Lewis and Clark reported on fertile land on the Pacific coast around the mouth of the Columbia River. Many Americans were prepared to go to war with Britain over British Columbia, but agreement was reached on the 49th parallel boundary. This left ample scope for colonization in the north west. The wagon trains which followed the Oregon trail brought farming families into this attractive region.

The South West. The new Mexican state claimed the whole of the south west of the country, from Texas to California and as far north as Utah and southern Wyoming. Spanish settlement had been based on missions which were often widely dispersed, and the non-Indian population of the region remained low. Between 1836 and 1847 the United States and Mexico were in an intermittent state of war, which ended with the capture of Mexico City and defeat for Mexico. Under the treaty the United States won the whole of the southwest. Existing property rights of the Spanish speaking people were, in theory, protected, but, in practice, they had no means of protecting them against the newly arrived 'Anglos', who controlled the courts.

Shortly before the treaty was signed, gold was discovered at Sutter's Mill in Northern California. This set off the Gold Rush, which brought fortune hunters flocking to California from the east, and, indeed, from many parts of the world. The influx of population in turn created a farming boom and California was rapidly converted from a thinly populated region, largely consisting of mountains and desert, to the world's most rapidly expanding economy.

Immigration.

From Europe. Any measurement of the population rise of Europe from the middle of the 18th to the end of the 19th centuries should properly include, not only statistics on those countries themselves, but also of the millions who emigrated to destinations in many parts of the world – as well as their descendants. Figures can not be collated, but people of European stock took over great areas of the world, often at the expense of the indigenous population.

In order to overcome human reluctance to disrupt living patterns, there needs to be a 'push factor' propelling people from their homes, and a 'pull factor' drawing them to a new environment. As in the early years of colonization, the growing wealth of the United States drew economic, political and religious refugees from Europe. The British still came. Many of the Mormons who pulled their handcarts across the plains to Utah originated from among the cotton mills of Lancashire. The depopulation of the Scottish glens provided a new stream, although most preferred to go to Canada. The Catholic Irish, angered by English protestant rule and by unjust land laws had long been ready recruits; the disastrous potato famine of 1845-6, which is estimated to have claimed the lives of a million people, turned the stream into a flood.

People now came from new countries of origin. Norwegian families, long accustomed to extremes of climate, left their marginal fiord farms to farm in the harsh environment of Wisconsin and the Dakotas. Germans fled from the political and social upheavals of their country. Peasants from southern Italy, condemned to live on the brink of subsistence under rapacious landlords, took the boat to America. Towards the end of the century, people were coming from further east. Russian Jews fled the pogroms; Poles fled Russian oppression. All funnelled through Ellis Island to emerge, often penniless, and speaking no English, onto the streets of New York. They worked as they could, in clothing sweatshops, on construction, in domestic service. Each new national group faced discrimination as those who were settled in jobs and homes tried to protect their position from the work-hungry newcomers.

The New Immigration. The capture of the south wes

brought a significant Spanish speaking population within the United States. Civil war in Mexico and an increasing divergency of the standards of living brought an increasing number of immigrants across the border. Most came as migrant workers, following the crops into California and far beyond. In good times, they were welcomed as cheap labour, but in times of depression they proved easy targets for discrimination. In the 20th century immigrants from Puerto Rico and other Caribbean islands have also increased the Hispanic population of the eastern side of the country.

Asian immigration began when Chinese labourers were recruited to work in the 1849 Gold Rush. Distinctive in those early days in their 'queues' and national clothing, they found themselves at the bottom of the immigrant 'heap', increasingly shut out from desirable employment and property ownership by Chinese Exclusion Acts. They, like subsequent Asian immigrants, preserved a respect for education, which enabled them to improve their status rapidly when the legal discrimination was brought to an end.

The United States Abroad.

The Continent. The Monroe Doctrine was originally proclaimed to protect emerging Latin nation seeking to establish independence from European colonial powers. In the later years of the century it was used to promote the continent as a sphere of U. S. interest.

One major thrust lay through the Caribbean towards South America. In 1903 effective control over the Isthmus of Panama was wrested from Columbia and the Panama Canal linking the two oceans was opened in 1914. War with Spain in 1898 also ended with the acquisition of Puerto Rico and Cuba.

American interests also led expansion across the Pacific. Alaska was purchased from Russia in 1867, providing the westward bridge of the Aleutian Islands. Midway Island was won in the same year, followed by Samoa and the Hawaiian group. The war with Spain finally brought Guam and the Philippines within the American empire.

Although the United States was no longer a new country, the need to absorb waves of immigrants fostered an introversion and at times an aggressive nationalism. Many American statesmen, wishing to distance their country from what they saw as the destructive quarrels of the old world, proclaimed a policy of isolationism. The history of the 20th century was to show that the world's greatest power could not successfully stand back from international events.

11. The Age of Imperialism.

ndia.

The East India Company. The battles in the 18th century between rival trading companies were fought, not to win territory, but to establish trading advantage. In 757, however, the British East India Company's army n Bengal first captured the French trading station and hen defeated the Nawab's army at Plassey. The company then found itself, by default, the inheritor of Mogul ower. Now irretrievably involved in politics, it gradually extended its control over large areas of the ub-continent.

Company officials never lost sight of the fact that heir objective was to turn in a profit. As the company xtended its control over all internal as well as external ade, the standard of living of many Indians declined. ompany officials took the opportunity of amassing rivate fortunes, often by corrupt means. In the days efore steam ships and the opening of the Suez Canal, dia was far distant from home. Men travelled out as bachelors and many took local women and lived much as Indian princes.

After the American revolution, the British government was reluctant to become involved in further colonial expansion. To bring the Company under control, however it assumed dual control of the Indian possessions in 1784 The writings of Adam Smith had discredited the old mercantilist ideas, which had been the justification for early colonization. In line with prevailing doctrines of free trade, the company therefore lost its monopoly trading rights and was reduced to an administrative organization

Modernization. The evangelical fervour of the age brought protestant missionaries of many denominations to the sub-continent. Most had a simple desire to replace the traditional religions of Hinduism and Islam. They started schools which offered western education and encouraged converts to adopt western dress and habits These missionaries looked to the Christian rulers for protection and active encouragement.

The new generation of administrators was less directly motivated by the profit motive and more by a desire to bring the benefits of modern life to the people of India. Many had a genuine, albeit paternalistic, respect for Indian culture, and they resisted the missionaries attempt to overturn traditional ways. These administrators did, however, believe in reform. Laws, based on western practice, were introduced to stamp out trad tional practices, such as the burning of widows and the killing of infant girls. The products of the industrial revolution, such as the electric telegraph and railways were also enthusiastically introduced.

The Mutiny. The modernisation programme inevitably created tension. Railways, for instance, were looked upon as a threat to the caste system. There was also powerful resentment against British acquisition of new land, particularly in the northern province of Oudh. The introduction of a new form of greased cartridge was the immediate cause of the Indian Mutiny of 1857. This was as much a traditionalist reaction against modernization as it was a rebellion against the ever expanding foreign rule. Many educated Indians, like the operators of the Delhi telegraph, died at the hands of the mutineers. The mutiny was put down with as much ferocity as it had been waged. The British parliament at last accepted direct responsibility for government. In 1877 Queen Victoria was proclaimed Empress of India and rule over the subcontinent became the symbol of British power. The true age of imperialism had begun.

The Raj. The new rulers determined that mistakes which had led to the mutiny should not be repeated. They therefore took care to respect the rights of the traditional ruling class. When early representative institutions were introduced, this ruling class was called upon to represent the Indian people. The aspirations of the rising intelligentsia were therefore overlooked. Indeed, the contempt for the educated 'westernized native' which was to be characteristic of British imperialism, was first shown in India. The first meeting of the Indian National Congress was held in Bombay in 1885, but a further 20 years would pass before independence appeared on the Congress agenda.

Throughout history, India, like China, had shown a capacity to absorb its conquerors; the British alone resisted assimilation. The new rulers of the Indian Civil Service were drawn from the elite and many acquired a knowledge of Indian language and customs, but, in the wake of the Mutiny, a barrier existed between the two races which could not be crossed. Fast and comfortable steam ships now linked Europe and India, and the journey time was much reduced when the Suez Canal opened in 1869. Administrators and traders increasingly kept their roots in Britain, while serving tours of duty overseas. Also men were now joined in India by their womenfolk. Few of these *memsahibs* had work which brought them into contact with Indian people, so their cultural values were never seriously challenged.

In the second half of the century new concepts of racial superiority were fashionable, particularly in northern Europe. Europeans had long treated other races as inferior, but they had not theorised about it. Now concepts of racial superiority were becoming fashionable partly based on popular Darwinianism. The European rulers of India, as of other colonized people, were therefore ill equipped to understand the nationalist aspirations when they did come to the surface.

China.

The Manchu Empire. In the middle of the 17th century, invaders from Manchuria overthrew the Ming emperor and established the foreign Manchu (Ch'ing) Dynasty. Following the ancient pattern, the early rulers were able men, who established a working relationship with the mandarin administrators, and for more than a century the land experienced one of its more prosperous periods.

By the end of the 18th century, however, problems were growing. It is estimated that the population trebled, from 100 to 300 million between 1650 and 1800, and it would reach 420 million by 1850. In China, Malthus' forecasts on the effects of population growth proved accurate. All available land was already under cultivation, so production could not match increased demand. The situation became disastrous in the terrible northern famine of 1887-9, when some ten million people starved to death. As social problems became worse, so the quality of imperial government deteriorated into corruption and mismanagement. Resentment boiled and people remembered that the Manchu were a foreign race.

In 1786 rebellion broke out in Shantung, and this was followed in 1795 by the White Lotus Uprising on the borders of Szechwan and Shensi. These were the preludes of a century of peasant unrest on a scale far beyond anything experiences in human history before that time. It is estimated, for instance, that more people died in the T'ai-p'ing Rebellion of 1850-64 than World War One, while huge Islamic risings of the north and south west left wide areas of the country devastated. The Manchu Dynasty, however, managed to cling to power through all these upheavals.

China and the West. Since the earliest times, China had always had a favourable balance of trade with Europe. There was a demand in the West of porcelain and silks, but, apart from a few clocks and toys, Europe had little to offer in return. Towards the end of the 18th century the balance took a turn for the worse. There was a fashion in Europe for Chinoiserie, reflected in some of the art of the period. More important, tea became the staple drink of many Europeans. This could only be bought by a steady drain of bullion.

Western merchants were convinced a huge Chinese market, was waiting to be opened up, but contact was strictly controlled through a few merchants in Canton. Attempts to open the market ended in frustration. In 1795 George III of Britain sent an emissary to the Manchu court with gifts. The Emperor thanked King George for his "submissive loyalty in sending this tribute mission" from "the lonely remoteness of your island, cut off from the world by intervening wastes of sea", but the mission achieved nothing of substance.

The Opium Wars. In the early years of the 19th century British traders found that the drug opium could right the adverse balance of trade. A great deal of Indian farmland was placed under the crop and the flow of bullion into China was quickly reversed. Apart from the direct damage done by the opium, the Chinese government found that the drain of wealth quickly created financial crisis. The opium trade was a breach of Chinese law, and in 1839 a large quantity was destroyed. In the following First Opium War the Chinese forces proved ill equipped to fight a modern war, and they were defeated. In 1842, China was forcedly opened up to foreign trade and missions, and Britain won control of the trading outpost of Hong Kong.

Thirteen years later, the British Prime Minister, Lord Palmerston, decided to assert British authority once again. His declared policy that half civilized governments such as those of China "all need a dressing every eight or ten years to keep them in order" made him popular at home. He was prepared to defend British citizens against the valid operation of foreign law and in 1856 he defied parliament to take Britain, with French help, to war with China again. The imperial army was weakened by the T'ai-p'ing Rebellion and in 1860 the allied army marched into Peking and burned the Imperial palace.

European Influence and Reaction. Although China herself remained nominally independent, her influence in Asia was much reduced. Russia used the British and French invasion as a cover for occupying the northern Amur river, so winning the Pacific outlet of Valdivostok; Britain won Burma, against fierce local opposition; France defeated Chinese armies to win Indo-China; Korea won its independence, later to fall to Japan; Japan conquered Taiwan; even the United States closed in by conquering the Philippines, again in the face of fierce nationalist resistance. Within China itself, the European powers jockeyed for privileges. Even more threateningly, the country was now open to western missionaries who, along with the Christian gospel, brought cultural assumptions profoundly at odds with traditional Confucian values.

The End of the Manchu Empire. By the last years of the century the ancient civilization was in collapse. In 1898 the young emperor and his advisers decided that China must follow the Japanese example and adopt western ways. The experiment was short lived as the dowager Empress led the faction of reaction. She imprisoned the emperor and gave support to the xenophobic Boxers, who were attacking mission stations and other western interests across the country, and the embassy area of Peking was besieged. The western powers replied by sending a combined army to relieve the city. Still the Manchu rulers clung to power, but they were threatened from two directions. The army war lords were now unreliable, and outside the country, young foreign educated men plotted to overthrow the dynasty. In 1911-2 the two combined to bring down the Manchu Dynasty. The foreign educated Sun Yat-sen became president, but one year later he gave way to one of the military commanders.

Japan.

The Shogunate. In 1603, at a time when the imperial family had lost effective power, the military leader, or Shogun, Tokugawa Ieyasu established power over the whole of Japan. In the centuries which followed, the Tokugawa shogunate closed Japan off from the outside world. The Japanese were prohibited from travelling abroad; Jesuit missionaries were expelled and their converts persecuted; only a few Dutch traders were allowed to operate from the city of Nagasaki. For Japanese urban entrepreneurs, however, the cost was a small price to pay for the peace and prosperity brought by the powerful shoguns. Educational reforms created a high level of literacy and a vigorous free enterprise economy was permitted to flourish in the growing towns. The growing prosperity of the towns was not matched in the country-side, where both the traditional lords, and the peasants tended to become poorer.

The Opening of Japan. In 1854 the navy officer, Matthew Perry, was commissioned by the President of the U. S. A. to open up the Japanese market. His Treaty of Kanagawa brought the years of isolation to an end. The shogunate did not long survive it, and the Emperor resumed direct power in 1868. There was now a fierce debate within Japan as to whether the country should adopt western ways wholeheartedly, or follow the example of China and remain separate. The reformers were able to point to the disastrous results of conservative policies, as applied in China. The largest feudal families voluntarily surrendered their rights and the government systematically set about the modernization of their country. The changes were based on the solid structure, bequeathed by the Tokugawa shogunate, but there remains no example in history of a comparable change in social life within a single generation. By 1900 an advanced system of state education had been constructed, western experts were imported to train the people in engineering, and young Japanese students were sent to study overseas. At first the new industries, like textiles and shipbuilding, were faithful copies of western proto-types, but they gained an increasing share in world markets. By the 1920s Japan was a formidable industrial competitor to the European nations.

Japanese Expansionism. The era of peace had left the samurai caste deprived of employment. They bequeathed an aggressive nationalism to the new state. The Japanese also recognized that European world domination had been based the use of force. The now popular motto 'Asia for the Asians' was intended as a Munroe Doctrine for a Japanese sphere of influence.

Russian power was particularly menacing. The transcontinental railway had now reached Vladivostok, and the Russians were showing interest in the newly independent Korea. In 1902 Japan concluded a treaty with Britain, which provided security against intervention and two years later she attacked Russian shipping in the Manchurian Port Arthur. The city fell in January of the next year and the Russian Baltic fleet was destroyed in the Tsushima Straits in May.

This victory of an Asian over an essentially European power in the Russo-Japanese War marked the end of the European military domination of the world, which had survived since the 15th century. In the years which followed, Japan continued to build an empire, first by the annexation of Korea and then by the acquisition of wide Chinese lands. These conquests were accepted as a fait accompli by the European powers at the Treaty of Versailles in 1919.

The Pacific.

The Aborigines of Australia. Some time before 50,000 years ago great ice caps in the polar regions made the world's seas lower than they are today. The Indonesian islands formed a great peninsula, and Australia was joined to Tasmania and New Guinea in a single land mass. At this time the ancestors of the Australian aborigines arrived in their isolated home. Despite the lower waters, they had still crossed a wide stretch of ocean making them possibly the world's first seafaring people. These early settlers brought their dogs, but the other animals would have provided a strange sight to people accustomed to the fauna of Asia. In their new home, they adopted a hunter-gatherer lifestyle, delicately in balance with the unique environment.

The Polynesians. Much later, some 4-3,000 years ago, a different race of people began to spread out across the islands of the Pacific Ocean. The methods by which they navigated their great canoes are little understood; they probably followed the paths of migrating birds, and it is suggested that they could feel the current off distant land masses on the surface of the water with their hands. Certainly they made successful voyages of up to 200 miles to colonize unknown islands. It appears that they went via Fiji and Samoa to the remote Marquesas Islands, from where they fanned out, north to Hawaii, south east to Easter Island and south west to New

Zealand, which they called Ao-te-roa, or Long White Cloud. The earliest settlers were probably fleeing from war, but in time warfare followed them to their new homes.

The Arrival of the Europeans. Australian aborigines and Polynesian islanders alike were for long protected from European ships by unfavourable trade winds. In the 17th century several Dutch sailors, operating from the East Indes, made voyages in the area, but they were not attracted by what they saw as the region offered no prospect of profitable trade. In 1770 the English Captain James Cook sailed along the east coast of Australia and landed at Botany Bay. He later commanded two more voyages through the Pacific Islands. The sailors found the Pacific island societies to be living examples of the noble savage' existence, extolled by writers such as Rousseau – and bequeathed the devastations of syphilis to the islanders.

Australia.

The Penal Colony. The war with the American colonies shut Britain off from the penal colonies of Georgia and the Carolinas, and so posed the British government with a problem of how to dispose of its surplus criminal population. As long as the war was in progress, convicts were kept in hulks, moored in river estuaries.

One of those who had landed off Cook's ship in Botany Bay was a geographer and scientist, called Joseph Banks. In the years which followed he had become the driving force behind an exploration movement, intended to open new areas of the world to British trade. Banks argued the case for establishing a penal colony in Botany Bay. The land was good, he argued, the climate mild and the natives few in number.

The first convoy sailed in 1787, under the command of Captain Arthur Phillip, carrying 571 male and 159 female convicts, supervised by over 200 marines. Most of those transported were hard core criminals, but there were also a significant number of political prisoners, particularly from rebellious Ireland. Large numbers of enforced immigrants suffered dreadfully on the long journey and in the penal settlements, and many continued to nurse resentment against the 'old country' and the forces of law and order.

Exploration. By the end of the century it was established that New South Wales in the east was linked to New Holland in the West in a single continent. In 1813 pioneers crossed the Great Dividing Range, which hemmed in the eastern coastal plain to discover the broad grasslands of the interior. By 1859 the landmass of the continent had been divided into six colonies.

It is said that, when these first white men appeared on the central plain, an aborigine scrambled into a tree and let out a long, high-pitched shriek. The establishment of European civilization in Australia was an immense achievement, but, yet again, the heaviest price would be paid by indigenous people in the age-old clash of interests between nomadic hunter-gatherers and settled agriculturalists.

Economic growth. The earliest settlers did not readily find cash crops to make the colony self sufficient. Lieutenant John Macarthur is credited with recognizing the immense potential of the interior for sheep farming. He developed new breeds which would flourish in the New South Wales grasslands and was able to live in the style of an English country gentleman. His example was followed by emancipated convicts and a new generation of free settlers. The influx of cheap Australian wool to the home country stimulated the Yorkshire woollen industry at a time when woollen fabrics were gaining popularity in world markets. Towards the end of the 19th century the development of refrigerated ships boosted the meat trade. Then, in the early years of the 20th century, strains of wheat were developed to suit the dry climate.

It was also early established that the continent possessed great mineral wealth. Gold and copper mines were in operation by the middle of the 19th century, and the great Broken Hills complex was opened up in 1883. Despite such development in the interior, the cities proved to be the main beneficiaries. By 1901, 65 per cent of the population lived in the six capital cities.

Political Development. Progress with self-government in Canada encouraged the British government to devolve increasing political responsibility in its colonies of European settlement. In 1901 the six colonies became states to form the Commonwealth of Australia. Old links proved decisive when Australian soldiers fought with the British army in the wars of the 20th century.

During World War Two, however, the nation's leaders, recognizing that Britain could contribute little against an expansionist Japan, turned to the United States for support. Since the war, extensive non-British immigration into Australia, and the increasing orientation of Britain towards Europe has further weakened traditional ties.

New Zealand.

European Settlement. In 1814 a group of missionaries arrived in the land which had been described by Captain Cook. It is estimated that, at that time there was a population of about a quarter of a million Maori people, who had lived in complete isolation for many centuries. In 1839 Edmund Gibbon Wakefield established the New Zealand Company, with a view to buying land off the tribes and organizing settlements. The British government, hoping to control the movement, formally annexed the country in the following year.

The British proclaimed equality between Maori and European people, but practice never matched theory, and the colonists' land hunger provoked the Land War of 1845-8. After further settlers arrived, many from Scotland, war broke out again in the 1860s. By 1870 the Maori people had effectively lost control of their land.

Constitution and Economy. The country was granted a constitution in 1852 and in 1907 it became a self governing dominion within the British Empire. Its dependence on agriculture, however, left it heavily dependant on the British economy. Early prosperity was based on wool and gold, but the introduction of refrigerated shipping in the last years of the 19th century favoured low cost New Zealand farmers, at the expense of their British competitors. This brought a period of prosperity, and ties with Britain were reinforced by disproportionate contribution made in two world wars. As with Australia, these have weakened in the second half of the 20th century, during which time the country has suffered from its heavy dependence on primary products.

Japan and The United States.

By 1914 Britain was withdrawing from direct involvement in the Pacific region but neither the emerging Australia or New Zealand were showing potential as a regional power. The Dutch still controlled the East Indes, modern Indonesia, but only at the cost of a series of major struggles against an emerging nationalism on Bali, Sumatra, and Java. Two power now faced each other; the United States, with forward bases in Samoa, Guam and the Philippines and the emerging power of Japan. The foundations of a major regional conflict were already laid.

North Africa.

Egypt. In classical times, North Africa had been an integral part of Mediterranean civilization. After the early flowering of Islamic civilization, however, it became increasingly cut off from the countries on the northern, Christian shore of the inland sea. Egypt was for centuries isolated under mameluke rule. When Napoleon led an army into Egypt in 1798, he took with him not only fighting men, but also scholars, who would be able to interpret the remains of the country's fabled ancient civilization.

French interest in the area survived the fall of Napoleon, and, when Mehemet Ali broke the power of the mamelukes and established effective independence from Ottoman rule, French influence remained powerful. Under Mehemet Ali and his grandson Ishmael, Egyptian power was taken south into the Sudan and along the Red Sea. Ishmael contracted with France for the construction of the Suez Canal, which was opened in 1869. He staved off financial collapse, however, by selling a controlling interest in the canal to Britain, who now controlled this lifeline to India. In 1881 the Egyptian government was threatened by a nationalist rising in Egypt and by the Mahdi in the Sudan, and Britain responded by sending a force to protect the canal. It was not intended as an army of occupation, but Britain became involved in a protracted war in the Sudan and a in administering a protectorate over Egypt.

Algeria. The coast of Algeria to the west was had long been the home of Barbary pirates. In the 1830s, France began a major advance into the area. The pirates were driven from their harbours, and the French moved south to the Atlas mountains. Here they met fierce resistance, led by Abd el Kadir, but they won control of the mountain passes. Military success was followed by an influx of French settlers into the coastal region.

Sub-Saharan Africa.

An Unknown Continent. For centuries the interior of Africa had been viewed by the outside world as little more than a source of human merchandise. European merchants had shipped slaves by the million out of the west coast; Bedu and Tuareg tribesmen had driven them across the Sahara to the markets of North Africa; they had been carried across the Red Sea in dhows by Arab traders; they had been beaten into submission by Dutch settlers in the south. The slave trade had had a profoundly brutalising effect on African life, far beyond the boundaries of foreign exploration.

Yet in the early 19th century, Africa had its own political movements. In the grasslands of West Africa, an aggressive Islam was expanding in Hausaland under the Fulani Uthman dan Fodio and in Futa Jallon, under Alhajj Umar. Far away, in the south west, the Bantu people were experiencing a period of unrest. Shaka founded the Zulu kingdom in 1818, setting neighbouring people on the move.

European Explorers and Missionaries. In the early days of the industrial revolution, there was a general view, vigorously fostered by Joseph Banks, that Africa was a land of unbounded wealth, which offered untapped opportunities for trade. Since Britain had most to sell, British interests funded the earliest explorers. Early explorers, such as Mungo Park, acted as commercial travellers, carrying samples of Lancashire textiles and other manufactures. Results were disappointing but some solid business was established on the coast in products such as palm oil.

By the middle of the century European interest was increasingly focused on 'the dark continent', and explorers, such as David Livingstone and H. M. Stanley became major celebrities. Livingstone maintained an interest in 'legitimate trade', which he hoped would displace the continuing traffic in slaves in Central Africa, but he travelled as a missionary. European civilization had now achieved an unassailable self-confidence. Romantic concepts of the noble savage were forgotten and it was readily assumed that Africa was in need of Christianity, Western customs, and the post-industrial working practices which alone could provide the basis for economic advance.

Explorers, mainly following the routes of the great rivers, penetrated deep into the continent. They were followed by missionaries from a wide range of denominations from Europe and America, who were at times almost as much at competition with each other as they were with traditional practice. Expectation of life for explorers, traders and missionaries in malarial West Africa could be measured in months until quinine was introduced as a prophylactic in the 1840s and even afterwards the coast was still considered unfit for European settlement.

The Scramble for Africa. In 1880 active European political interest in Africa was limited to the French colony in Algeria in the north and the British Cape Colony in the south. The old Portuguese colonies, various ex-slaving trading outposts and settlements of freed slaves retained only tenuous links with Europe. By 1914 in the whole continent, only Ethiopia was a truly independent nation. In the intervening decades the continent was divided up between colonizing powers. Lines were drawn on maps in European capitals; boundaries sometimes followed rivers, often placing a village in one country and its farm land in another. The colonizing movement was in places the focus of national policy; elsewhere it was the product of adventurers or commercial companies working on their own initiative.

The British assumption of control in Egypt provoked the jealousy of other European countries. In particular, the French army was suffering from the bitter humiliation of the defeat at Sedan in 1870. Africa offered a forum for the recovery of a lost military prestige.

France and Britain were the main protagonists in the northern half of the continent. French colonization followed two thrusts. The first came south across the Sahara from Algeria into the grasslands of West Africa. The second went east from Senegal along the upper Niger to Lake Chad towards the Nile. The British also had a dual thrust, south from Egypt and north from South Africa. The imperialist Cecil Rhodes dreamed of establishing an unbroken chain of British possessions from the Cape to Cairo. French and British forces met where the thrusts intersected at Fashoda in the southern Sudan in 1898, when for a time it seemed likely that the two countries would be involved in a colonial war.

Meanwhile the British had also established West African colonies, based on their old slaving stations. The Germans were active in West, South West and in East

Africa. King Leopold of the Belgians gained control of the Congo as a private venture. This was taken over by the Belgian state in 1908. Spain won control of much of the north western Sahara and shared influence in Morocco with France. Italy belatedly joined the scramble by invading Libya in 1911.

In the early years colonization was largely bloodless, but the process became increasingly violent. Britain faced African revolts as far apart as the Gold Coast and Rhodesia and France the Niger and Madagascar. The brutality of King Leopold's exploitation of the Congo was exposed in 1904. In the same year a major rebellion broke out against the Germans in South West Africa, which ended when they drove the Herero people to virtual extinction in the desert. The Italian invasion of Libya was also conducted with widespread brutality. By the beginning of 1914 the re-drawn map of Africa could be seen as a symbol of a dangerously aggressive and expansionist mood within Europe.

South Africa.

The Great Trek. During the Napoleonic Wars Britain occupied the Cape of Good Hope, and the territory was retained, as the Cape Colony, in 1814 for its strategic value in controlling the sea routes to the east. At that time, however, there were no British settlers, the land being shared between nomadic Bushmen and Hottentots and

Afrikaner speaking Boers of Dutch and French Huguenot origin. Soon the new government began to bring in
thousands of British settlers. The Boers were angered
when their black slaves were freed and laws were introduced which they considered to be unduly favourable to
the previously subject black people. In 1835 some 10,000
Boers left their homes at the Cape and settled on land of
the Vaal and Orange Rivers. More Boers followed when
the British annexed their republic of Natal. The settlers
set up the new republics of Transvaal and the Orange
Free State where they could live free from British interference.

The movement of the Boers from the south coin-
cided with migrations of Bantu people, displaced by the
Zulu kingdom. The two people clashed, but the main
losers were the native nomadic people, who were driven
to a precarious existence in the desert.

The Boer War. Resentment between Boers and the
British continued to grow. The British briefly annexed
the Transvaal, and, although they withdrew, this left the
Boers feeling that they would never be left in peace.
Then, in 1886, gold was discovered in the Transvaal, and,
within a few years, a new city of Johannesburg had
grown to a population of 100,000. Most of the newcomers were British, but they were excluded from the running
of the republic. Angry that the world's great empire, the
modern Rome, could be frustrated by a small number of

intransigent Boer farmers, Cecil Rhodes provoked a confrontation. President Kruger of the Transvaal, an implacable opponent of British rule, responded with an ultimatum, and war broke out in 1899.

Liberal opinion in Britain and Europe saw the Boers as an oppressed minority, and, when they were finally defeated in 1902, there was pressure for a generous settlement. A few voices were raised in the British parliament to defend the rights of the black peoples, but these found no support. In 1909 the four territories were brought together into the self governing Union of South Africa, which lost little time in passing laws which discriminated against the non-white peoples. In 1948 the Afrikaner speaking people won power within the country and put in place the formal structure of apartheid.

12. The Nation State in Crisis.

The Eastern Question.

The Decline of Ottoman Power. In 1683 armies of the Ottoman empire laid siege to the city of Vienna for the second time and Europe was threatened once more from the East. The armies withdrew, but the Emperor at Istanbul still controlled almost three quarters of the Mediterranean coastline – North Africa, the Arab lands of the Middle East, the homeland of Turkey, Greece and the Balkans.

By the 18th Century statesmen could recognize that the Ottoman Empire, like other empires before it, was in decline. Administration was clumsy, and the sultan had to rely on local rulers, whose loyalty was often in doubt. Also, the social military structure of the empire was becoming increasingly out of date.

Russian Objectives. Russian statesmen took the closest interest in the Ottoman decline. Peter the Great had won a warm water port, but, for both trade and strategic reasons, the country still badly needed an outlet into the

Mediterranean Sea. In 1768-74 Catherine the Great fought a successful war against the Turks and won the Crimea and other territory on the north bank of the Black Sea along with rights of navigation into the Mediterranean. She also established that Russia had the right to act as protector of eastern Christians within the Turkish dominions.

Russia continued too make advances after the defeat of Napoleon. She won control of the ancestral Ottoman homeland in the grasslands east of the Caspian Sea, aking her empire as far as the mountain passes of the Himalayas. Still further east, she won the Pacific port of Vladivostok from the Chinese. Russian territorial ambitions were backed by huge military forces, and other European powers perceived her as an aggressive imperial power.

Concern focused on the fate of the Turkish European territories. In a private conversation with the British ambassador, Tsar Nicholas 1 described Turkey as 'the sick man of Europe'. He implied that it would be better for the powers to consider how to share the sick man's possessions, rather than to wait and fight over them when e died. Other powers, however, preferred to support Turkey so that it could continue to act as a check on Russian ambitions in Eastern Europe.

In 1841 the European powers came together in the Convention of the Straits to guarantee Turkish independence. It was agreed then that the Bosphorus should be closed to all ships of war. This shut Russia out of the Mediterranean, and meant that she could not protect her merchant ships, now carrying increasing grain exports by the Black Sea.

The Crimean War. In 1851 Russia invaded Turkey's Danube lands, and in 1853 her navy sank the Turkish fleet, so winning back her outlet to the Mediterranean. Excitement ran high in Paris and London. Napoleon III was looking for a way of rebuilding the family's military prestige. Britain was concerned for her links with India for, although the Suez Canal was not yet built, traffic was already following the Mediterranean route. In March 1954 the two powers declared war on Russia in support of Turkey. Combined forces were despatched to capture the Russian naval base at Sevastopol in the Crimea. The huge Russian army was unable to dislodge the invading force and in 1856 she was forced to accept peace on the terms that she would keep no fleet in the Black Sea and build no bases on its shores.

The battles of the Crimean War were made famous because the armies were followed by a journalist, who published detailed reports in the London *Times*. For the first time in history, the public was able to read first hand reports of the sufferings of the soldiers. The modern profession of nursing dates itself from the work done by Florence Nightingale and her staff in this campaign.

Disintegration. Victory over Russia in the Crimean War could not long delay the final disintegration of the Ottoman Empire. France and Britain, who had fought as allies of the Turks, were happy to help themselves to territory in North Africa. Britain also occupied Cyprus and extended her influence in the Middle East. Russia continued her forward movement in the less sensitive territory to the east of the Caspian Sea. In Eastern Europe, Greece was already independent and in the half century after the end of the Crimean War, Serbia, Rumania and Bulgaria would also break free. Russia, always ready to stand as protector of the oppressed Slav peoples, went to war with Turkey again in 1877. For a time Europe stood on the brink of another war as the powers prepared to shore up the tottering empire once again. In 1878, however, Russia, faced by the combination of Prussia, Austria and Britain, was forced to accept terms at the Congress of Berlin.

In 1907 rebellion broke out in Turkey itself. A group, who called themselves the Young Turks, demanded constitutional reforms, along European lines. In 1909 the long reigning Abdul-Hamid was deposed. The new rulers dressed their government as a constitutional monarchy, but it was effectively a dictatorship, dedicated to reviving Turkish power, at home and in the remaining Ottoman lands of the Middle East.

Nationalism.

Western Europe. The Napoleonic conquests and the reactions against them had aroused fierce emotions of nationalism, which were to influence European politics. Germany and Italy began their discovery of a national identity (Chapter 8), but the mood also affected smaller peoples, such as Belgians and Norwegians. Britain had her own problems in Ireland. The situation was complicated by the fact that Westminster politicians had to reconcile two vocal nationalist groups. The majority Catholics considered themselves to be under a foreign power, discriminated against in their religion and insecure in their land holding. The minority Protestants of the north, mostly of Scots descent, used their political connections with English conservatives to defend accustomed privileges. After 1848, however, concern on issues of nationality centred on eastern Europe.

Poland. Russia might stand as the liberator of oppressed Slav peoples in the Balkans, but, on her own western frontier, she was the oppressor. The decline of Poland began with long wars against Sweden, which ended in 1709. Depopulated and weakened, with no natural frontiers, she stood between aggressive powers to east and west. In the last decades of the 18th century, she was partitioned between Russia, Austria and Prussia. A supposedly free Poland, created in 1815, was effectively a Russian colony. A series of nationalist rebellions were a failure and Russian administrators tried to eliminate all traces of Polish nationalism, insisting that even primary school children should be taught in the Russian language.

The Austro-Hungarian Empire. Metternich recognized very clearly that the new nationalism could undermine the whole structure of the Austrian empire. The house of Hapsburg ruled over different nationalities, speaking a wide range of languages. Defeat by Prussia and then the loss of Italy pushed the western boundaries of the once great empire back to the Austrian heartland. Alone of all the major European powers, land-locked Austria was not in a position to participate in the scramble for colonial possessions. Any expansion had to be towards the east, and foreign policy now focused on the Danube and the Balkans.

The new nationalists of the region, however, saw Austria, as much as Turkey as a threat to their aspirations. The Hungarians exploited the weakness of the Empire after the Prussian victory at Sadowa to negotiate a new Covenant with Vienna. The Hapsburgs now ruled a dual Austro-Hungarian empire, in which military and foreign policy was co-ordinated, but in other ways the eastern part had virtual self government. The new Hungarian section of the Empire contained a number of national minorities, and trouble was never far from the surface.

In 1878, after the war between Russia and Turkey,

Bosnia and Herzegovina were placed under Austrian administration, and in 1908 they were annexed by Austria. The independent Serbia, with Russian support, now stood as the focus of pan-Slavic aspirations, and so as protector of the nationalist movements in the two territories. The Austrian government, angry at this subversion, looked for an opportunity of crushing Serbia.

Russia.

Despotism. In the decades before the Crimean War, Russia was ruled by the autocratic Tsar, Nicholas I. He tried to keep all western ideas of liberalism and socialism at bay by a suffocating censorship. At the same time the administration became ever more corrupt and inefficient. The repression of this period was primarily directed against the intelligentsia, who were traditionally close to developments in the west. Nicholas did recognize, however, that the position of the serfs had become such an anomaly that it endangered the Russian state. As in France before the Revolution, these poorest people had to carry by far the bulk of the load of taxation. Nicholas declared a desire to make changes and he did make progress in codifying peasants' rights and bringing them within the legal system. He was unable, however, to tackle the medieval structure of serfdom, which tied the mass of the people to their villages, and left them as the virtual possessions of their masters.

Emancipation and Reform. Nicholas was succeeded by his son, Alexander II during the Crimean War. The failure of the superior Russian armies and the humiliating nature of the peace, left no doubt that the state needed radical overhaul. Although conservative by nature, the new Tsar supervised a major overhaul of the army, the law and the administrative system.

Most difficult, he put in train the process of emancipation for the serfs. "Better," he said, "to abolish serfdom from above, than to wait till it begins to abolish itself from below. " Emancipation was pronounced in 1861, but problems still remained to be solved. Landlords needed to be compensated and a system had established whereby the peasants could buy their own land. This took the form of a tax, which left many, in practice, worse off than they had been before emancipation.

The Prelude to Revolution. The first shot was fired at Alexander only five years after his emancipation decree; he was assassinated in 1881. The reforms of his reign were matched with a continued autocracy, which aroused profound frustration, particularly amongst the intelligentsia. The education system, in particular, was subject to the tightest control by a reactionary bureaucracy. During these years also individuals within government gave support to pogroms against the Jews. After the murder of Alexander in 1881, government fell increasingly into the hands of the opponents of reform.

223

Opposition was divided between liberals, socialists and groups of nihilists, all of whose leaders were drawn from the intelligentsia. They appealed first to the suffering peasants, demanding a programme of land reform. Towards the end of the century, however, large numbers of peasants were leaving the land to make up the industrial proletariat of the long delayed industrial revolution. Revolutionary activists now found it productive to work in the growing slums of the cities, building up revolutionary cells of workers.

Success is the ultimate justification of autocratic government, and defeat by Japan in 1905 brought the imperial government to the brink of collapse. The battleship *Potemkin* mutinied and terrorised the Black Sea. Massive strikes, particularly by railway workers, crippled the economy. In October 1905 the Socialist groups organized themselves into the First Soviet, based on the principle of the cells which had been established in the factories. Nicholas II, like Louis XVI before him, was forced to attempt to rally national unity by calling a national parliament, or *duma*. Experiments in representative democracy were, however, half-hearted and failed. In the years which followed, the weak Tsar shut himself increasingly within his family circle, now increasingly dominated by the eccentric Rasputin. When the European war broke out in 1914, Russia was ill prepared for such a disaster.

The Armed Peace.

The Alliances. In the years after 1871, there were two fixed points in European diplomacy. Austria and Russia faced each other over the control of the liberated Turkish lands in the Balkans. Fighting could break out at any time within the region, leading to the risk of 'superpower involvement'. France also, smarting from defeat at Sadowa and the occupation of Paris, was chronically hostile to Germany. She was, however, militarily weak and the autocratic powers of Austria and Russia looked on her as a threat, and so she remained isolated and impotent.

In previous centuries, alliances had been formed under the immediate threat of war, and they had disintegrated immediately after the threat was over. During these decades, however, the European powers began to form themselves into permanent alliances, committed to help each other in the event of war. By the beginning of the 20th century, a new alignment of powers had become established. Germany allied with Austria, and they were later to be joined by Italy to form the Triple Alliance. To meet this threat, France and Russia joined to form the Dual Alliance. Britain was not a significant continental power, and as late as 1898 the two countries narrowly avoided a colonial war. In 1904, however, policy changed dramatically as Britain concluded a non-binding *entente cordiale* with France, which was followed by a similar

225

agreement with Russia. Hostility towards Germany increased as the German government set about a major naval construction programme, which was interpreted as a direct threat to Britain. The British government responded with its own programme, and a major arms race was under way.

Military Strategy. With Europe organized into armed camps, the generals considered strategy in the event of conflict. Failing to take account of the bloody attrition of the American Civil War, they assumed that events would be settled, as in Bismarck's wars, by one swift, decisive campaign. Germany was faced with the prospect of fighting on two fronts. Strategists decided that, while the Russian war machine was massive, the bureaucratic inefficiency would prevent rapid deployment of forces. They therefore developed a plan that, in the event of impending war, the German army would make a first strike to knock out France, so that it could then give full attention to the eastern front.

In the early years of the century, there was a mood of militarism throughout Europe, fed by accounts of colonial wars and victories against non European people. It was most evident in Germany, where theorists declared that war was the natural state of man, but it spread much wider. In Britain, for instance, metaphors of war and sport were subtly mingled in the public school education of the nation's elite.

The Outbreak of War.

Austria and Serbia. By the summer of 1918 Serbian support for rebels in Bosnia and Herzegovina had brought relationships with Austria to a low state. On the 28th June the heir to the throne, the Archduke Franz Ferdinand and his wife were murdered in the Bosnian capital of Sarajevo. Encouraged by her ally Germany, Austria used this as a pretext for invading Serbia. On the 30th July Tsar Nicholas II ordered mobilization, not only in the Balkans, but along the whole border.

First Strike. It appears that, at the last moment, Kaiser Wilhelm II of Germany may have had doubts about plunging Europe into war. The British foreign minister tried to gather support for a conference to localize the conflict, but the German war machine was now moving under its own impetus. On the 3rd August Germany attacked France through undefended neutral Belgium. Italy declared that the conflict was none of her concern, so the central powers of Germany and Austria faced France and Russia. Britain had no treaty obligation to enter the war on behalf of France, but did consider herself bound by guarantee the guarantee made to Belgium after the 1830 uprising. Her formal position for taking up arms was therefore as defender of the rights of small nations. Italy later entered the war on the side of the Allies, as they were now called, while Turkey and Bulgaria aligned themselves with the Central Powers.

Military enthusiasts forecast a short war, to be decided by Christmas, but the British Foreign Secretary, Sir Edward Grey warned, "The lamps are going out all over Europe. We shall not see them lit again in our lifetime. "

War and Revolution.

Stalemate. The German first strike strategy involved high risk. Russia mobilized more rapidly than anticipated the and German army was defeated at Grumbinnen on the 20th August. In early September the western offensive became bogged down on the Marne. Germany was fighting the war on two fronts, which her generals had feared. On the western front, the opposing armies dug in for their long years of attrition. The new German navy remained in port as the British fleet set about sapping German resistance by blockade. Allied attempts to break the stalemate by offensives in the Dardanelles and Salonika, were unsuccessful.

The Russian Revolution. The huge open spaces of the eastern front kept war more mobile. Early Russian success was undermined by the failure of the political structure. In March 1917 a wave of unrest swept the Tsar from power. The opposition was divided between liberal politicians, who now set up a provisional government and the socialist Soviet – itself divided between the moderates and a radical Bolshevik wing. The moderate provisional government pledged itself to continue the war, but in April the Bolshevik, Vladimir Ilyich Lenin, returned from exile and announced the arrival of world revolution. Russian workers, he claimed, should not be dying in a bosses' war. The provisional government staked every-thing on a last great offensive, but this failed, and on the 7th November, Lenin staged a Bolshevik coup d'état. In March 1918 he concluded peace between his newly born Soviet Union and the Central Powers at Brest Litovsk.

American Intervention. Germany now had to fight on only one front, but, during this period, another, even more formidable enemy had been drawn into the war. Desperate at the success of the British naval blockade, the German navy mounted its own submarine blockade of Britain. To be successful it had to attack American ships which were carrying supplies to Britain. This brought the United States into the conflict in April 1917. The German High Command recognized that the intervention of American troops would tilt the battle against the Central Powers, but it staked everything on defeating Britain and France before the Americans arrived. 1917 and 1918 saw huge and costly offensives from both sides on the western front. In the Autumn of 1918 Germany's allies, Austria and Bulgaria began to crumble, the German fleet mutinied and there was increasing unrest in the German cities. Finally the Kaiser abdicated and the generals sued for peace.

The World of Versailles.

The Cost of War. All the major continental nations emerged weakened from the war. Russia, involved in civil war, was no longer a factor in international politics. France, though victorious, had suffered grievously. Austria was now not a power of significance. Germany, although defeated, was no longer surrounded by serious rivals. Loss of life had been severe in all the combatant nations, but wealth had also drained away. The United States was the main beneficiary of the war at a cost of fewer casualties than had been suffered by the Dominion of Australia. In the past she had been a major debtor nation, but now she moved into a period of being the world's main creditor.

A New World. The war was also an emotional and intellectual landmark. It was as if the great optimism, which had buoyed up a successful and expansionist Europe was suddenly pierced. The belief an inevitable tide of progress, prevalent since the time of Descartes, no longer seemed tenable in the face of sustained barbarity on European soil. Liberal thinkers, in disciplines such as theology as well as in politics, found themselves on the defensive. New absolutisms, of both left and right, emerged in confrontation, both threatening to overwhelm traditions of representative government.

The conflict had also brought permanent changes in the structure of society. Women, who had been mobilized to fill men's jobs, could no longer be denied political and a growing economic emancipation. The war brought technological advances in areas such as aeronautics and the development of motor vehicles. Output had increased to meet the demands of a technological war, and, in the process, labour unions had established a stronger position for themselves. Many felt threatened by the rapid social change, evident in almost every field of life.

In the years before the war, artists had already been working in strange and disturbing new forms. Stravinsky's *Rite of Spring* and Picasso's *Demoiselles d'Avignon* created scandal in their fields. In 1922, Joyce's *Ulysses* dispensed with the convention of the English novel. It seemed as though all recognisable values were now fractured as creative artists abandoned both classical and romantic forms to explore abstraction and an inner life, now provided with a whole new vocabulary by the works of Sigmund Freud. The arrival of jazz from America, exploiting the interaction between African and European popular music, only served to heighten the alarm of traditionalists.

The Treaties. The Treaty of Versailles, ratified by Germany in July 1919, was the first of a series of treaties imposed on the defeated Central Powers. The leading architects of the new order were President Wilson of the U. S. A., Clemenceau of France and Lloyd George of

Britain. Clemenceau, recognizing the continuing potential of Germany, pressed for financial reparations, intended to retard industrial recovery, the return of Alsace-Lorainne to France, and the demilitarisation of the Rhineland. The map of eastern Europe was re-drawn, with Poland, Hungary, Czechoslovakia and Yugoslavia created as new nations. In the north, Finland, which had won independence from Russia in 1917, was joined by the three newly independent Baltic States. The pattern of nationalities was, however, more complex than could be accommodated within national boundaries, and all of these nations had substantial minorities. Of greatest significance for the future, substantial numbers of German speaking people found themselves within Czechoslovakia and Poland. The treaties attempted to protect minority rights, but there was considerable movement of peoples across national boundaries. The largest movement came at the end a war between Greece and Turkey from 1920 to 1922. In particular Greek people left the coast of Asia Minor, where they had lived since ancient times. The two communities continued in uneasy co-existence in Cyprus.

The treaties also changed the wider world. Germany's East and West African possessions were divided between Britain and France, while South West Africa, the future Namibia, was placed under the trusteeship of South Africa. The concept of trusteeship was also used to

232

extend western influence over the old Ottoman territories of the Middle East.

The League of Nations. President Wilson hoped that his country, with its democratic tradition could take the lead in creating a new atmosphere of goodwill. He therefore proposed a League of Nations, which would serve as guardian of world peace. Wilson was to be bitterly disappointed when his own Congress refused to let the United States join the new body. Unhappy about the way in which their country had ben plunged into European affairs, the majority of Americans were anxious to return to a traditional isolationism. It became evident that the new body lacked credibility as early as 1920, when Poland successfully seized Vilna from Lithuania. Later incidents reinforced the fact that successful international collaboration to repel aggression could not be organized through the League. The Italian government took full advantage when, in Europe's final African venture, it launched an attack on Ethiopia in 1935.

Ireland. Attempts by pre-war liberal administrations to give home rule to Ireland had been frustrated by the collaboration of Ulster protestants and conservative politicians. Prime Minister Lloyd George now faced destructive guerilla warfare from nationalists. In 1921 the moderate nationalists accepted partition of the island, which left a significant Catholic minority within the Protestant dominated northern provinces. This led to civil war within the new Irish Free State, and laid the foundations of continuing strife in the north.

The World Economy.

The Post-War Boom. During the 1920s world trade appeared to be returning to its pre-war vigour, but, even during these boom years, there were signs of problems ahead. The war had created an increased potential for production, but demand was stagnant. The Soviet Union was in no position to import goods from abroad, and new nations raised tariff barriers to protect fledgling industries. The United States now produced over half of all the world's manufactures, but American consumers, like the Japanese 70 years later, showed little desire to buy goods from abroad and domestic industry was protected by import duties.

As industry boomed, so the price of raw materials, including agricultural products, declined, creating problems for primary producers. At the same time, the fact that workers did not share the profits of their industries, brought outbursts of industrial unrest, such as the British General Strike of 1926.

The Great Depression. By 1928 world trade had become heavily dependant on American finance. In that year Wall Street experienced The Great Bull Market as the price of shares rose to unrealistic heights. Then, on October 28 1929, the stock market crashed. American capital for investment dried up, leading to a rapid world wide collapse of industrial confidence. Governments took what action they could to protect their own industries against imports, so further inhibiting world trade. It is estimated that at the depth of the recession in 1932 industrial production in the United States and Germany was only half of what it had been three years earlier. Unemployment reached record levels in all the industrial countries, bringing times of great hardship.

The New Deal. In America, the parties divided over the political response to the problems. The Republicans, favouring a traditional *laissez-faire* approach, were defeated in the 1932 elections by a Democratic party, led by Franklin Roosevelt. He instituted a New Deal, based on substantial public investment. The showpiece was the publicly owned Tennessee Valley Authority. Designed to provide an industrial infrastructure for one of the country's poorest regions. Roosevelt won great popularity, going on to win an unprecedented four presidential elections, but the improvement brought by the New Deal was as much psychological as practical, and real recovery had to await the stimulus of a second world war.

The Rise of the Dictators.

Italy. In the elections of 1921 a new party won just 36 seats in the Italian parliament. Its leader, Benito Mussolini had a background as a socialist, but he now proclaimed that he would save Italy from the menace of communism. The party appealed to ancient Rome in its extended arm salute and the symbol of the *fasces*, which gave the movement its name. The black shirted fascists used intimidation, first to come to power and then to eliminate all political opposition. Mussolini's rule achieved some legitimacy when, in 1929, he negotiated a treaty with the highly conservative papacy.

Germany. The Austrian born Adolf Hitler became leader of the German National Socialist, or Nazi, party in 1921. Having failed in an early attempt to take control of the Bavarian government, he set about reorganizing his party as a military movement, not hesitating to purge his own followers. He directed his appeal to a German people, who were frustrated by military defeat, humiliated by the loss of empire and European territory, and, in many cases, impoverished by hyper-inflation. Hitler's philosophy was laid out in his early book *Mein Kampf*. This described both his military ambitions for Germany, and his obsessive hatred of the Jewish people.

The struggle appeared to lie between Hitler's new right, and the parties of the left. But the left was divided. The communists, taking their orders from Moscow, attempted, and sometimes succeeded, in fomenting revolution. The social democrats were therefore forced into alliance with conservative military leaders. Capitalizing on these divisions and on the economic problems brought by the Depression, Hitler took his Nazi party to power in 1933. He then quickly set up a reign of terror. While the Jews were the prime target, political opponents, gypsies, the handicapped, and anybody not considered to be of true Aryan descent also suffered. Despite this, his popularity remained high among most Germans. His armaments and other public works programme appeared to be bringing a return of prosperity, while military success retrieved national pride.

The Soviet Union. The Bolshevik revolution of 1917 was followed by three years of civil war, during which White Russian armies, supported by foreign troops, tried to overthrow the new communist state. Lenin and his followers emerged successful, but at huge cost. It is estimated that some 13 million died in the war and the famine it caused; economic life was at a standstill. In 1921, as a emergency measure, Lenin largely freed the economy and recovery followed rapidly.

Lenin died in January 1924, leaving two men contending the succession. Trotsky proclaimed that the new society could only flourish within a communist world, and the prime task was therefore to export the revolution. His opponent, Stalin, argued that the priority was to rebuild the Soviet Union, by creating 'communism within one state'. When Stalin emerged victorious, it appeared as though the forces of moderation had prevailed.

Stalin assumed autocratic power and created a personality cult, not dissimilar to those constructed around the fascist dictators. He set himself the objective of changing the Soviet Union from a largely medieval economy, to a major modern state within a few decades. This involved the conversion of agriculture from its peasant structure by wholesale collectivization, and the rapid development of heavy industry. The programme was forced through at huge human cost. Industrially the results were dramatic. Production of coal, iron and steel and other basics increased many times over. The expansion of heavy industry was, however, bought at the expense of consumer goods, and the people, were constantly disappointed in the promised general improvement in living standards. Peasants on the collective farms, also resentful at being expected to produce low cost food for the growing cities for little return, remained obstinately unproductive.

Stalin's increasingly paranoiac behaviour was now demonstrated in a series of show trials and purges. Virtually all the old political leaders and a high proportion of military officers were executed to ensure that nobody would be able to challenge for power. Millions more suffered and died in labour camps. The new administrators of the country were tied to Stalin by a common guilt, and by an increasing web of petty corruption.

Spain. By the 1930s the days in which Spain had been a great European power were long past, and she had therefore avoided involvement in the First World War. In 1933 a right wing government came to power, which provoked rebellion by national minorities. In early 1936 a left wing government was elected with a large majority. General Franco, modelling himself on the fascist dictators, led a mutiny of the army in Morocco and invaded the mainland. The army, the political right and the Roman Catholic church aligned with Franco, while left wing groups and the national minorities aligned with the elected government. Franco received assistance from the fascist states, while the government was supported by the Soviet Union and a variety of international volunteers. The bitter war lasted until 1939, when Franco achieved the position of dictator, which he held until his death in 1975.

The Second World War in the West.

German Expansion. From the beginning Hitler, followed a programme for the creation of a German empire in central Europe. His first objective was to win back land lost at Versailles; he then planned to conquer the whole of mainland Europe, including European Russia, and create an empire in which 'lower' races, such as the Slavs, would be reduced to a servile status. He exploited the weakness of the League of Nations, American isolationism, and lack of unity among other European powers in a series of successes – the recovery of the Saarland by plebiscite, the remilitarisation of the Rhineland, unification with Austria, and finally the dismemberment of Czechoslovakia. When Britain and France acquiesced to the last of these at Munich, it appeared as though no other power had the will to frustrate his ambitions.

In 1939 Hitler and Stalin concluded the Nazi-Soviet Pact to preserve Russian neutrality. The Soviet Union was awarded eastern Poland and took the opportunity to advance further into the Baltic States and Finland, where Russian armies were halted by fierce national resistance. Unlike Czechoslovakia, Poland was protected by treaty links with Britain and France, and the German invasion provoked a joint ultimatum and war. Mussolini took the opportunity of entering the war in support of Germany and invading Greece.

German Successes. After defeating Poland, in 1940, the German army repeated the 1914 tactic of invading France across Belgium. This time Paris fell and a puppet government was installed in southern France. Successful campaigns to the north and south reduced Denmark, Norway, Yugoslavia and Greece. In early 1941 the Afrika Corps landed in Libya and within two months was threatening Cairo and the Suez Canal. Britain, now rallied by the charismatic leader, Winston Churchill, held off an air offensive, intended to prepare the way for invasion, in the Battle of Britain.

On 22 June 1941 Hitler launched Operation

Barbarossa against an unprepared Soviet Union. The invasion followed the logic of Hitler's master plan, but it dangerously overstretched German resources. The imbalance was made greater when the Japanese attack on Pearl Harbour brought the United States into the war in December of the same year. Stalin demonstrated his character as a national leader in rallying his people for a massively costly defence. The war turned in November 1942, when the Russians broke the German front at Stalingrad and a British army defeated the Afrika Corps at El Alamein. Once the Allies had re-established a western front with the Normandy landings of June 1944, the final defeat in 1945 was inevitable.

The years from 1939-45 gave a new and terrible meaning to warfare. The Germans mobilised conquered people for slave labour, and perpetrated mass genocide on European Jewry; the Russians deported whole national populations for alleged collaboration; residential areas of cities were targeted in indiscriminate bombing by both sides. Among some 50 million dead were an estimated 27 million Russians, 6 million Jews and $4^1/_2$ million Poles.

Europe Divided.

The Yalta Settlement. The future political shape of Europe was negotiated in February 1945 at a conference at Yalta in the Crimea, attended by Stalin, Roosevelt and

Churchill. Germany was to be partitioned and the countries of Eastern Europe were to form a zone of Russian influence. In the event, Austria and Greece – the latter after civil war – remained within the western sphere.

The Recovery of Western Europe. At the end of the war, western Europe was in a state of serious economic collapse. Once again, there were large movements of displaced people, and food shortages continued for years after the war. In June 1947, the U. S. Secretary of State, George Marshall, announced a major aid programme, directed, "not against any country or doctrine, but against hunger, poverty, desperation and chaos". The Soviet Union was offered the chance of participating but turned it down. The Marshall Plan provided much needed capital for reconstruction.

The United Nations. During the last years of the war, thought was given to the reasons why the League of Nations had failed to preserve world peace. In 1945 representatives of the nations met in San Francisco to set up the new United Nations. In its constitution, great influence was given to the Security Council, which had five 'great powers' as permanent members and representatives of other nations. The right of veto given to the great powers, but at least all the major powers were now involved in the organization and debates were subject to the scrutiny of the world media.

The European Community. Some European leaders

now argued that the nation state was no longer capable of providing a secure structure for world peace. In particular, the long standing enmity between France and Germany was no longer tolerable. In 1952, the Federal Republic of Germany, France, Italy, Holland, Belgium and Luxembourg, formed the European Economic Community. This was designed to be both a trading group, capable of competing with the new super-powers, and also a stabilizing influence on the volatile European political scene.

The Cold War in Europe. It soon became clear that European nationalism had run its destructive course, and the danger to world peace now lay in the confrontation of the United States and the Soviet Union. In the words of Winston Churchill, an 'iron curtain' had descended across Europe.

The Soviet Union emerged from the Second World War in control of a vast empire. It had inherited imperial conquests, and had further added the Baltic Republics. It also now controlled puppet regimes in Eastern Europe, bound together in the Warsaw Pact, which maintained huge land forces on its western front. Stalin's policy was still primarily directed at preserving national security, which had been so devastatingly violated by Hitler's army. He and later Soviet leaders therefore felt threatened by American superiority in nuclear weapons. A crash nuclear programme was put in hand and advances in rocketry were clearly illustrated when, in April 1961,

Yuri Gregarin became the first man to be launched into space.

America and her allies in the North Atlantic Treaty Organization (NATO) relied heavily on nuclear superiority. The Americans responded to the Russian space programme and, in July 1969, with a wondering world watching on television, men were placed on the moon.

Berlin, divided between the four occupying powers, lay exposed within the Russian area of influence and in 1948-9 conflict loomed as the Russians shut off western communications with the city. A later crisis ended with the building of the Berlin Wall in 1961. This stood for the next 28 years as a potent symbol of the Cold War and the division of Europe into two hostile camps.

13. After Empire.

The Expansion of Japan.

The Beginnings of Aggression. The 1914-18 war brought prosperity to the rising Japanese economy. European competition in Asian markets was reduced and Japanese factories were able to export to the combatants. During this period, heavy industries, such as shipbuilding, were able to build up a firm base. Competition returned in the post-war boom years, but Japan continued to export successfully. During the boom years, companies re-invested profits in preparation for more difficult times. Japanese industry, none the less, suffered badly in the Depression. With foreign markets closed and the home market as yet undeveloped, industry worked at only a fraction of capacity. The weakness was exacerbated by the country's lack of raw materials. Foreign policy therefore became directed at the winning control of the export markets and natural resources of East Asia. China was the first target for expansion.

China's Weakness. After the fall of the Manchu Empire in 1912, China plunged back into chaos. Sun Yat-

Sen's Nationalist (Kuomintang) party struggled for power with independent war lords. During this time communist cells were coming into existence. Following Marxist orthodoxy, they initially concentrated on the cities, but later, under the influence of the rising Mao Tse-tung, they worked increasingly among the mass of the peasants, who had suffered greatly during the upheavals. Under his influence, the communists built up communes in scattered and remote areas. Sun Yat-Sen died in 1925 to be succeeded as Kuomintang leader by the more conservative Chiang Kai-shek. After a period of collaboration, Chiang attempted to exterminate the communist opposition. Driven from their southern bases, the communists only survived by coming together in the Long March of 1934-5 and establishing a new northern headquarters, based on Yenan.

The War in the East.

The attack on China. Japan exploited the weakness and growing corruption of the Kuomintang government by strengthening its control over Manchuria and areas of the north in the early 1930s. In 1936 the Kuomintang and the communists made common cause against the foreigners, but in the following year, Japan launched a major assault on China. In December 1937 the Japanese army captured the capital at Nanking and the Chinese government had to retreat to remote Szechwan, leaving the Japanese in control of the north, and most of the Pacific coast, including the major industrial cities.

Victory brought Japan into conflict with the Pacific colonial powers, and their concessionary ports were blockaded. The Americans and British responded by supplying Chiang Kai-shek along the Burma Road, and the United States renounced its commercial agreement with Japan.

Control of the Pacific. Japanese foreign policy was now set on winning control over the whole of the Pacific rim. With the outbreak of war in Europe, she allied herself with Germany. Then in 1941, as German troops were sweeping into Russia, she launched her first attack on French Indo-China. On the 7th December 1941 her air force attacked the American navy in Pearl Harbour, Hawaii, and, at the same time, she launched assaults on the Dutch in Indonesia and the British in Mayalsia and Burma. The campaigns were brilliantly successful and by mid 1942 both India and Australia were under threat.

Defeat and the Atom Bomb. The attack on Pearl Harbour put and end to isolationism and united Americans behind President Roosevelt. As the world's greatest industrial power became geared for war, the tide turned against Japan. In June 1942 the Japanese fleet suffered a reverse at the battle of Midway Island, and thereafter a relentless American offensive drove them from their Pacific conquests, while the British also fought back through Burma. From November 1944 the Japanese cities came under direct air attack. The war ended with the use of the new atomic weapon on the cities of Hiroshima and Nagasaki in August 1945.

Decolonization. The Japanese victories, and, in particular, the fall of Singapore on the 15th February 1942 involved a profound loss of face for the colonizing powers. The invading armies were seen by many Asians as liberators from western regimes. Many of those who had assumed control, under Japanese direction, now became prominent in independence movements. The United States handed over political control of the Philippines in 1946 after negotiating a continued military presence. The Dutch, themselves newly liberated, at first fought to preserve their possessions but in 1948 they accepted the independence of the Republic of Indonesia. The British fought a communist rebellion in Malaya before handing over to a more acceptable national government in 1957. The French became involved in a long war for Indo-China before being defeated in 1954.

China and her Neighbours.

Communist China. The fall of Japan left the two forces of the Kuomintang and the communists vying for the control of China. China's miseries continued when civil war broke out in 1947. In one battle, half a million men were engaged on each side. By 1949 the communi nists were gaining the upper hand and in May 1950 Chiang Kai-shek retreated to Taiwan with his government.

The new communist government was faced by a huge task of reconstruction. According to Mao's estimate, some 800,000 'enemies of the people' were executed, largely from the old village landlord class. The communists had long experience with the collectivization of agriculture within their own territories, and they did not follow Stalin's example of imposing it from above. Peasants were organized to control their own operations and, despite set-backs, the conditions of life for the mass of people improved.

Mao Tse-tung capitalized on the age-old Chinese respect for authority to provide a strong central government, which had for so long been lacking. He adapted western Marxist ideology to traditional thought patterns, and showed a strong hostility to western culture, which was given full rein in the Cultural Revolution, which he launched in 1966.

To western eyes, China appeared now to be a part of a united Communist bloc, intent on achieving world dominance. In practice, however, Mao had largely rejected the Russian brand of communism. By the 1960s, acute strains were appearing in the relationship between the two countries. When China developed its own nuclear capability in 1964, it was primarily as a deterrent against potential Russian aggression. The Chinese reconquest of the old province of Tibet also led to a successful war with India in 1962.

The Korean War. In 1945 the Japanese colony of Korea was occupied by Russian troops from the north and Americans from the south. This led to partition, with both governments claiming the whole country. In 1950 the northern armies invaded the south. The United States and other western nations, with the backing of a United Nations resolution, responded by sending forces to support the south.

For a time it appeared as though the north would be defeated, but China, concerned at her own security, sent an army across the border. The American President Truman refused to become involved in a war on Chinese soil, and the war was concluded in 1953 by an armistice which perpetuated partition.

Conflict of Ideologies. American analysts saw the communist strategy in South East Asia and being a process of 'slicing the salami'. Territories were to fall to communism, not in one major conflict, but one by one. The communist uprisings, which faced almost every nation of South East Asia in the coming decades, were in fact little co-ordinated and variously owned allegiance to Moscow, Peking or neither. That in the new nation of Indonesia was put down with great violence.

American policy became dedicated to holding the

line against communism in the region. This involved providing support to non-communist regimes, including Chinese nationalist government in Taiwan. The United States was therefore deeply involved in the politics of the region.

The French defeat in Indo-China left the new country of Vietnam divided, with a communist regime under the old nationalist Ho Chi Minh established in the north. The United States became increasingly involved in the struggle, supporting unstable non-communist administrations, based in the southern capital of Saigon. In 1965, faced with the possibility of the defeat of the client regime by the northern backed Viet Cong guerillas, President Johnson authorized massive involvement in the conflict. The weight of American firepower proved ineffective against a highly motivated enemy. In 1973 the American government, confronted with a mounting anti-war campaign at home, withdrew from the conflict. In the next two years the three countries of Indo-China fell to the communists. The people of Cambodia, having experienced American bombing, now suffered from the worst aberrations of Marxism, as interpreted by the Pol Pot regime.

The Pacific Rim.

Japanese Reconstruction. United States troops occupied Japan, in an enlightened manner, from 1945 until

1952. The first objective was to ensure that the expansionist phase was over. A new democratic constitution was established, the Emperor renounced his divinity, and expenditure on defence and armaments was radically curtailed. As with Germany, industrial reconstruction followed fast. After the humiliation of defeat, both nations needed to experience success. Also, the imposed limitation of defence expenditure proved a powerful boost to the civilian economy.

The Technological Revolution. Soon Japan was no longer a low cost economy and her heavy industries began to suffer some of the problems experienced in the West. By this time, however, the nation had developed skills, which enabled it to take the lead in the third, technological phase of world industrialization. Automobile production boomed, winning markets in Europe and North America, and Japanese labour and management skills proved highly suitable to the detailed work involved in the production of hi-tech goods. Supported by a huge balance of payments surplus, she has established a position of dominance in world markets in a wide range of product areas.

An Area of Growth. In the last decade of the 20th century it is clear that the region of the Pacific rim is established as a formidable competitor to the established industrialized regions of western Europe and North America. It remains, however, a region of wide diversity.

South Korea, Taiwan, Singapore and – at least until re-unification with China in 1997 – Hong Kong have participated in the economic prosperity pioneered by Japan. At the other extreme, peoples of many of the nations of South East Asia continue to survive on low per capita incomes. China herself emerged from the isolation of the Cultural Revolution to re-build international links, but, unlike communist regimes to the west, it has successfully repressed those who wished to liberalize the political structure of the nation.

The Indian Sub-Continent.

The Independence Movement. Indian troops made a significant contribution to the allied victory in the World War One, and in 1918 nationalist politicians looked to see their country start its progress towards the self government which had already been given to the white dominions. In 1919, however, a British general ordered troops to fire on a demonstration in Amristar, killing some 400 and injuring many more. Although the government disavowed the act, many British residents were loud in support, fuelling bitterness between the two communities. One of those radicalised by the Amristar massacre was Mohandas Gandhi, known as Mahatma (Great Soul). During the next decades, he led a civil disobedience movement, based, if not always successfully, on non-violent principles.

In the face of opposition at home, as well as from residents in India, the British government slowly moved towards accepting the principle of granting dominion status to India, and the Government of India Act of 1935 gave substantial power to elected representatives. The movement for complete independence, however, continued to grow. With the outbreak of the World War Two, some Indians sided with Japan in the hope of bringing down the colonial power.

Partition. The independence movement still faced the problem of reconciling the two major religious groupings of the sub-continent. Mohammed Ali Jinnah emerged as leader of the Muslim League, which now demanded that an independent state of Pakistan should be established at independence for the Islamic community. In 1945 a Labour government was returned in Britain and in March 1946 it made an offer of full independence. As disputes continued, it announced that Britain would withdraw not later than June 1948. Faced with this ultimatum, the Hindu leaders accepted partition – for which decision Gandhi was assassinated by an extremist Hindu.

The new state of Pakistan was established in two blocks in the north west and north east. The rulers of princely states on the boarder of the two nations were permitted to decide their allegiance, leaving Kashmir as disputed territory. Independence was marked by com munal rioting, which left some half a million dead, and the mass movement of peoples in both directions across the frontier.

Independence. Jinnah died in 1948 and a decade later the army took control of Pakistan. Leadership of India fell to Jawaharlal Nehru and later passed to his daughter, Indira and grandson Rajiv Gandhi. The new country faced formidable problems. Independence was quickly followed by famine in 1951, and, with rising population it appeared as though Malthusian disaster was imminent. A combination of a reduction in the rate of population growth and an agricultural 'green' revolution has, however, improved the supply of food. The fragile ecology of eastern Pakistan, however, continued to bring disasters and a cyclone in 1970 led to rebellion, which, with Indian help, brought into being the separate Islamic state of Bangladesh.

Partition did not bring the end of India's communal problems. Indira Gandhi was assassinated by discontented Sikh nationalists, and her son Rajiv by Tamils of the south. Mahatma Gandhi allied himself with outcasts and hoped to see the end of the caste system, but this has been frustrated by a resurgence of Hindu fundamentalism. For all its problems, however, India remains the world's largest democracy.

Sub-Saharan Africa.

Decolonization. British governments of both parties continued the policy of giving independence to colonies which had begun with India. The sheer size of the British Empire had meant that expatriate manpower was spread thinly. The second layer of administration was already staffed by African personnel and a machinery of local government was in place. Riots in the Gold Coast in 1948 gave notice of a growing nationalist movement. In 1957 the Gold Coast became the first independent country within the British commonwealth, under its new name Ghana. Three years later the much larger Nigeria became a sovereign state.

Across the continent, in Kenya and Rhodesia the problem was complicated by the presence of a white settler population, bitterly opposed to any move toward majority rule. The most serious challenge was posed by the Mau Mau disturbances in Kenya of 1952-6. Many of the white minority left the country when it received its independence in 1963. Two years later the white minority government of Southern Rhodesia declared unilateral independence and seceded from the British commonwealth. The British government failed to take effective action against this colonial rebellion and war continued between the white government and black nationalist groups, until the latter won to set up the state of Zimbabwe in 1976.

French governments, disillusioned by prolonged war in Indo-China and Algeria, gave independence at an even faster pace. In 1960 the Sub-Saharan colonies were offered either complete separation, in which case, they would receive no continued assistance, or association with France, within a French Community.

The two largest African empires were therefore dismantled within a few years with comparatively little strife. Independence for the remaining colonies proved a more painful process. In 1960, the Belgians withdrew from the Congo, which became the state of Zaire. Until that time, Africans held no positions of responsibility, and there was little preparation for the event. When the mineral-rich area of Katanga attempted to secede, the Cold War super-powers became involved in the ensuing civil war.

The last African empire was also the oldest. The Portuguese colonies of Guinea Bissau, Mozambique and Angola only achieved independence after prolonged struggle.

After Independence. The emergent nations faced formidable problems. Some new nations spent unwisely on and military prestige projects, but, even where this was avoided, as, for instance, in Tanzania, falling world commodity prices led to a serious reduction in government revenue. Industrialization has proved unattainable, both through lack of capital, but also because it has proved hard for products from new nations to break into the controlled markets of the developed world.

Independent African nations found themselves caught in the Malthusian nutcracker of increasing population and falling revenue. This led to a decline in already low living standards and a failure by governments to deliver the public health and education programmes expected within a newly liberated nation. This exacerbated traditional communal rivalries, which in turn frequently erupted into civil war, like the Nigerian Biafra War of 1967-70 and later struggles in the Sudan, Ethiopia and the Horn of Africa. Political instability led to the emergence of authoritarian, often military, regimes. An already difficult situation has been made worse for nations immediately south of the Sahara by climatic change and desertification, which have destroyed large areas of productive land.

South Africa. The violently imposed apartheid system led to South Africa being increasingly ostracized from the world community. She withdrew from the British Commonwealth in 1961, and was later expelled from the United Nations. Economic sanctions imposed by the U S. A. and a world sporting boycott had an effect and in the early 1990s the legal apparatus of apartheid was dismantled, but, with the white community continuing to control the police and armed forces, the political structure of a future multiracial nation remains unresolved.

Latin America.

Capital and Industrialization. In the years before World War One there was heavy European involvement in the economy of Latin America. The war then led to a drying up of European capital and the United States became the main investor in the region.

The world depression of the 1930s hit the region hard. The price of primary products, which were the mainstay of the economies, collapsed. After the war many of the larger nations instituted industrialization programmes, at times with a measure of success, but this was achieved only by borrowing the required capital, which left the nation with a heavy burden of debt and vulnerable to currency and interest rate fluctuations on the international market.

Economic problems created political instability. The rural poor had always lived in conditions of poverty, but they did not pose the same immediate problem to political stability as the growing and highly volatile urban populations.

Political Structures. The economic problems of the region meant that reforming governments did not have the revenue to deliver the social programmes needed to combat deprivation. When reforms were attempted they created inflation which weakened the economic base of society. Reforming democracies have therefore been under constant pressure from more authoritarian sys-

tems of government. These took three broad forms –
popularist leaders, military regimes and revolutionary
governments.

The archetype polularist leader was Getulio Vargas,
who came to power in Brazil in 1930, and the best known
Juan Peron, who ruled the Argentine from 1943-55 and
then returned briefly in 1973. Both drew comparison
with European dictators, but they had wide support
among the urban poor, who believed that they alone
could take on powerful vested interests on behalf of the
people. They depended, however, on army support, and
both were vulnerable when this was withdrawn.

Cuba and Revolution. The revolutionary movement
had early roots in Mexico, but it became focused on Cuba
with the success of Fidel Castro's revolution in 1959. An
attempt by the United States to undermine the revolution
came to disaster at the Bay of Pigs in 1961. In the
following years Cuba, now aligned with Russia, ex-
ported revolution into Latin America. Che Guevara, a
symbol to the new left across the world, was killed
fighting with Bolivian guerillas in 1967. The United
States became involved, supporting anti-communist regimes within the region, even when these had a poor
human rights record. The democratic left wing government of Salvadore Allende in Chile, for instance, was
overthrown by the military in 1973 with American support. Contra rebels against the Cuban inspired governmen

of Nicaragua were funded from Washington, and the government of the island of Grenada was overthrown by American invasion in 1983.

The Missile Crisis. In 1962 Cuba was the focus of the most dangerous crisis of the Cold War. In October intelligence reports showed that sites were being built on Cuba from which missiles would be able to reach any city in the United States. President Kennedy demanded that all missiles in Cuba should be withdrawn and announced that ships bringing more would be intercepted. The super-powers stood poised for nuclear confrontation, but the Russian President Khrushchev broke the crisis by agreeing to withdraw the missiles. President Kennedy had successfully reasserted the Munroe Doctrine that the American continent would remain an area of United States influence, and the powers would not again come so close to open war.

The Middle East and North Africa.

The New Turkey. In 1918, a proposal was put forward that Turkey itself should be divided into French, British and Italian spheres of influence. The successful general, Mustafa Kemal, led resistance against Greek and French forces, and established independence for the new, smaller nation. He set about a process of modernization of the nation, which went as far as westernizing its script and converting the country into a secular state. His people gave him the name of Ataturk – father of the Turks.

The Mandates. The old Ottoman lands of the Islamic Middle East, now finally separated from the Ottoman Empire, had acquired new strategic importance with the early development of oil reserves – although the scale and future importance of these were not as yet recognized. National boundaries were drawn up and the region was divided between France and Britain under the mandate of the League of Nations. This implied that the newly defined countries were destined to move towards self governing status. France was awarded Lebanon and Syria, although she had to take possession of the latter by force, and continued to rule it with considerable oppression. Britain received Palestine, Iraq, and Trans-Jordan, and she also controlled the emirates of the Persian Gulf. In 1932, Britain largely withdrew from Iraq, but the Palestinian mandate turned out to be something of a poisoned chalice.

The Founding of Israel. The objective of founding a Jewish national home in Palestine was first put forward in a Zionism Congress as early as 1897. It was to be a refuge for Jewish people who were persecuted in the pogroms of eastern Europe, and it also attracted many from minority Jewish communities within the Arab world. In 1917, the British government gave support to the project, with the contradictory provision that it should not interfere with the rights of the indigenous people. The movement was given further impetus by German persecution of the Jews under Hitler. In the post war years, large numbers of European Jews sought entry, and the British authorities had the impossible task of reconciling the opposing interests. In 1947 the United Nations voted for the partition of Palestine in the face of opposition from the Arab states and in 1948 the British withdrew. In the ensuing war, large numbers of Arabs left their homes for refugee camps in the neighbouring countries. The Arab states refused to accept the existence of a Jewish state in the Islamic heartland. The refugees remained, unsettled, waiting to return to their homeland as Israel and her neighbours continued in a state of war.

North African Independence. After World War Two the British presence in Egypt was restricted to a defensive force in the canal zone and, by 1956, Libya, Tunisia and Morocco had shaken off foreign ties. Armed conflict centred on Algeria, where over one million French settlers resisted any move towards independence. The country was declared an integral part of metropolitan France and a bitterly fought dispute continued from 1954-62. When General de Gaulle finally decided to give independence, colonists allied with army generals and France itself was taken to the brink of civil war.

Nasser and Pan-Arabism. In 1952 a group of Egyptian army officers overthrew the monarchy. Two years later, Gamal Abdel Nasser became president of the country. His objective was to establish Egypt as the unquestioned leader of a new and more coherent Arab people. Lacking oil resources, however, Egypt remained a poor country and Nasser planned a development programme based on the construction of the Aswan High Dam on the Nile. When the Americans and British withdrew offers of funding, Nasser turned to the communist bloc for support, so introducing cold war politics into the Middle East.

In 1956 he nationalized the company which administered the Suez Canal. In October the Israelis invaded Egyptian territory, ostensibly to destroy guerilla bases and this was followed by a joint attack by the British and French on the Suez Canal zone. World opinion was outraged, and the American government applied pressure which forced the invaders to withdraw.

The Suez fiasco left Nasser as the leading figure within the Arab world, but his attempts to take this towards political union were unsuccessful. In 1967 he closed the Straits of Tiran to Israeli shipping and the Israeli army launched a 'first strike' in what has become known as the Six Day War. After a successful campaign, Israel controlled new territory, including, from Jordan, the whole West Bank of the River Jordan, and, from Syria, the tactically important Golan Heights. Jerusalem, a city of great symbolic importance to all three Semitic religions, now passed under full Israeli control. Successive Israeli governments, in time reinforced by the possession of nuclear weapons, have failed to comply with United Nations resolutions demanding withdrawal from the occupied territories. Indeed, increasing numbers of Jewish immigrants have been established in West Bank settlements. As Israel's neighbour, the Lebanon, collapsed into civil war, many Arabs resorted to international terrorism.

The Oil Crisis. In 1961 Britain withdrew from her interests 'east of Suez'. Much of the, now increasingly vital, oil production of the region, however, remained under the control of western companies. A further outbreak of hostilities between Israel and her neighbours in 1973 led the Arab countries to 'play the oilcard' by taking more direct control over their own reserves and withholding supplies from Israel's allies in the developed world. This led to an increase in price, which had a sharp effect on the world economy. The Arab nations, and other oil producing nations, led by Saudi Arabia now organized themselves into O.P.E.C., with a view to controlling world prices. This was less successful than had been anticipated because the depression caused by the price rise restricted world demand, and Britain and Norway, opening new North Sea reserves, stood outside the cartel.

In 1978 Nasser's successor, President Sadat, made peace with Israel under American sponsorship at Camp David. This did not end the conflict within the region, but rather took Egypt out of the mainstream of Arab politics.

Iran and Islamic Fundamentalism. With Egypt returned to the American sphere of influence after Camp David, the Soviet Union turned increasingly to the radical, though mutually hostile, governments of Syria and Iraq. The United States, looking for a buffer between the Soviet Union and the oil-rich Middle East, put heavy backing behind the conservative and corrupt administration of the Shah of Iran. In 1979 discontent erupted into revolution, and the Shah was replaced by a fundamentalist regime, dominated by the Ayatollah Khomeni. This sparked a wave of Islamic fundamentalism which gave expression to pent up Arab anger at the imposition of alien values by aggressive western societies. Equally hostile to capitalist and to communist ideologies, Islamic fundamentalism has threatened governments of different complexion from Afghanistan to Algeria. Indeed, the failure of the 1979 Soviet invasion of Afghanistan in support of a crumbling Marxist regime, demonstrated militant Islam to be a highly effective barrier against further Russian expansion in the region.

Iraq. In 1979 Iraq came under the full control of a determined and ruthless leader, Sadaam Hussein. He had ambitions to revive Nasser's pan-Arab vision, this time based on Iraqi military power. He received wide western and Arab backing when he took his country to war with Iran, but he failed to achieve any of his war objectives. In 1990, he attacked and occupied Kuwait, provoking an international response in 1991, which left his country damaged, but his own power intact.

The Collapse of the Russian Empire.

Cracks in the Structure. As early as 1953, the year that Stalin died, there were signs of unrest among subject people of the Russian Empire. Yugoslavia, while remaining communist, had already loosened her ties with the Soviet bloc. Anti-Soviet riots in East Germany in 1953 and in Poland in 1955 were followed by rebellion in Hungary in 1956. The last was suppressed by military force, launched under the cover of the Anglo-French attack on Suez. The profound unpopularity of Russian domination and of the repressive puppet regimes continued to be demonstrated by a haemorrhage of refugees crossing from East to West Germany. In 1961 the East German authorities responded by building that ultimate symbol of the Cold War – the Berlin Wall. In 1968 a reforming communist government in Czechoslovakia was again overthrown by Soviet tanks. By this time large Russian forces were also tied down on the eastern frontier to check an increasingly hostile China.

Collapse. Meanwhile the government was coming

increasingly under strain within the Soviet Union. Khrushchev's denunciation of Stalin at the Twentieth Congress of the Soviet Communist Party and the termination of the worst excesses of the secret police enabled citizens to express dissatisfaction. Industrialization had been bought at the expense of the production of consumer goods, The corrupt and petty bureaucracy was increasingly exposed, and agriculture remained in the disastrous condition bequeathed by Stalin's collectivization.

In 1985 President Gorbachev inherited a collapsing empire. Constricted by domestic pressures, he chose not to intervene when, in a few dramatic months of late 1989 and early 1990, communist governments of Eastern Europe collapsed under popular pressure and new regimes declared themselves independent of Soviet control. The tearing down of the Berlin Wall, and subsequent reunification of Germany was the most powerful symbol of change. The situation was little better in the republics which constituted the Soviet Union. The people were increasingly dissolutioned by falling living standards and inefficient government. Powerful nationalist forces, from the southern republics of Armenia to Azerbaijan to the old Baltic States in the north now threatened to break up the Soviet Union from within. In August 1991 an attempt by communist 'hard-liners' to restore the old system in a coup d'état failed, leaving the central Soviet government stripped of any real power. As one republic after another announced secession it was quickly clear that the world possessed another 'sick man' – with all the attendant dangers.

The collapse of the Russian Empire at least signalled the end of super power confrontation. Faced with mounting problems at home, Gorbachev looked for support from America and other western nations and the Strategic Arms Limitation Treaty of July 1991 began the long process of disarmament. The benefits for world peace were illustrated when the Soviet Union refrained from backing Iraq in the Gulf War, so preventing a regional conflict being inflated into a confrontation of superpowers. At the time of writing, the formidable problems of the Soviet Union itself, and of the emerging democratic states of Eastern Europe remain unresolved, but the fear of the human race being destroyed by its own weapons has – rightly or wrongly – been overtaken by new environmental concerns, which centre on the rate in which post-industrial man is consuming the natural resources of the planet.

284